Regulating the European Environment

Second Edition

Wiley Series in
ENVIRONMENTAL LAW

Campbell/International Environmental Law Volume 1
1996 0–471–95229–X 300 Pages

Enmarch-Williams/Environmental Risks and Rewards for
Business
1996 0–471–96437–9 256 Pages

Garbutt/Environmental Law: A Practical Handbook Second
Edition
1995 0–471–95226–5 208 Pages

Garbutt/Waste Management Law Second Edition
1995 0–471–95227–3 280 Pages

Grant/Concise Lexicon of Environmental Terms
1995 0–471–96357–7 256 Pages

Lister/EU Environmental Law
1996 0–471–96296–1 328 Pages

Robinson/Public Interest Perspectives in Environmental Law
1995 0–471–95173–0 376 Pages

Forthcoming Titles

Burton/Water Law
0–471–96577–4 240 Pages

Jones/Environmental Liability
0–471–95554–X 280 Pages

Regulating the European Environment

Second Edition

edited
by

Thomas Handler, BA, LLB
(Sydney)
Baker & McKenzie

JOHN WILEY & SONS

Chichester · New York · Weinheim · Brisbane · Singapore · Toronto

Published in 1997 by John Wiley & Sons Ltd,
        Baffins Lane, Chichester,
        West Sussex PO19 1UD, England

        National 01243 779777
        International (+44) 1243 779777
        e-mail (for orders and customer service enquiries): cs-
        books@wiley.co.uk
        Visit our Home Page on http://www.wiley.co.uk
                    or http://www.wiley.com

Other Wiley Editorial Offices

John Wiley & Sons, Inc., 605 Third Avenue,
New York, NY 10158–0012, USA

VCH Verlagsgesellschaft mbH, Pappelallee 3,
D-69469 Weinheim, Germany

Jacaranda Wiley Ltd, 33 Park Road, Milton,
Queensland 4064, Australia

John Wiley & Sons (Asia) Pte Ltd, 2 Clementi Loop #02–01,
Jin Xing Distripark, Singapore 129809

John Wiley & Sons (Canada) Ltd, 22 Worcester Road,
Rexdale, Ontario M9W 1L1, Canada

IMPORTANT DISCLAIMER
The material in this volume is of the nature of general comment only. It is not offered as advice on any particular matter and should not be taken as such. The firm, the editor and the contributing authors disclaim all liability to any person in respect of anything and the consequences of anything done or omitted to be done wholly or partly in reliance upon the whole or any part of the contents of this volume. No reader should act or refrain from acting on the basis of any matter contained in this volume without taking specific professional advice on the particular facts and circumstances in issue.

The law is stated as at 1 July 1996

British Library Cataloguing in Publication Data

A catalogue record for this book is available from the British Library
ISBN 0–471–97167–7

Typeset in 10/13pt Garamond from the author's disks by Intype London Ltd
Printed and bound in Great Britain by Biddles Ltd, Guildford and King's Lynn.

This book is printed on acid-free paper responsibly manufactured from sustainable forestation, for which at least two trees are planted for each one used for paper production.

THE EDITOR

Thomas Handler was born in Budapest, Hungary, and graduated from the University of Sydney, New South Wales, Australia, with degrees in Arts and Laws. Admitted as a solicitor in New South Wales and in England, he became a partner of Baker & McKenzie in 1973. He established the environmental law group of Baker & McKenzie's London office and acts as coordinator of the environmental law group of the firm's European offices. His environmental law practice is for companies in the UK and elsewhere and includes a broad range of general corporate, liability and disputes issues. He is also involved in commercial dispute resolution work and in Hungarian issues.

Thomas Handler is a senior associate of the Foundation for International Environmental Law and Development. He is chairman of Environmental Resolve and a director of The Environment Council. He is a member of the Executive Committee of the Environmental Law Foundation. He is a trained mediator accredited by the Centre for Dispute Resolution and trained and practises as a mediator with Mediation UK's Camden and Haringey Mediation Services.

Thomas Handler has written many articles on environmental law and the resolution of commercial disputes and edits the Baker & McKenzie environmental law newsletters of the London office and the international firm. He has collaborated on publications on environmental issues by the Economist Intelligence Unit and the British Institute of Management and is legal consultant to the Environmental Law Foundation periodic publication *ELFline*. He has spoken many times at conferences in the UK, Europe and the USA on environmental law, product liability and the resolution of commercial disputes.

BAKER & McKENZIE

Baker & McKenzie is an international law firm, dedicated to advising businesses. It is the largest law firm in the world, with a worldwide network of 55 offices and representative offices in 34 countries, including 23 in Europe, plus a European Co-ordination

Centre in Brussels. The firm is therefore in a unique position to report and advise on the national and international aspects of environmental law and of its relevance to businesses. Baker & McKenzie has active environmental law groups, including international and European groups, making their transnational and local expertise available to clients worldwide.

It is Baker & McKenzie environmental lawyers practising in the relevant jurisdictions who have written the individual chapters and collaborated to produce this book.

Preface

This book is addressed to those engaged in business. They, like everyone else, have seen "environment" become an important word in daily affairs, with public and political forces, both national and international, generating much regulation of the environment. Regulation of the European environment is likely to continue, with increasing momentum and variety.

Environmental regulation can touch businesses with opportunities in the marketplace, but also with new responsibilities and burdens. Understanding these is a difficult and time-consuming task, but one that is also important and rewarding. With the sweep of regulation so broad and complex, those engaged in business might legitimately ask: "Where do I start?"

This book aims to give an introduction, providing an initial understanding of the general shape of the mass of rules and legislation in Europe. It is not intended to be exhaustive or to be a substitute for advice in specific cases, but aims to provide a basis for further detailed analysis of the subject if required.

The framework set out in this book can be relevant to significant areas of business operations, such as:

- corporate environmental policies, including management, purchasing, operations and energy use;
- acquisitions and disposals of businesses or shares, including necessary enquiries, audits, warranties and indemnities;
- policies and terms of lending, financing and insurance;
- acquisitions and disposals of land, including audits, site surveys, enquiries, warranties and issues concerning contaminated land;
- authorisations to operate and consents to discharge;
- pollution control, including waste minimisation, disposal and recycling;
- health and safety of employees and others;
- production and disclosure of information, including infor-

mation required to be given to regulators and under schemes such as eco-labelling and eco-management and auditing;
- civil, administrative and criminal liabilities (and their enforcement) arising from non-compliance with legal requirements during operations or from accidents;
- the impact of new regulatory approaches, such as new relationships with governments and regulators, charging schemes and taxes.

Although it is national legislation that is generally most directly relevant, European Community (EC) law is increasingly important. This book therefore contains an outline description and analysis of the environmental laws and some current developments in the EC and in Belgium, the Czech Republic, Egypt, England, France, Germany, Hungary, Italy, Kazakstan, the Netherlands, Poland, Russia, Spain, Sweden and Switzerland.

Environmental regulation continues to develop fast. Whilst account has been taken of developments since the last edition and of some that are current, it is hoped to refine and develop this publication further in the years to come.

Readers' questions, suggestions or comments about this book are therefore particularly welcome. Readers who have them or who would like further information on any subject covered in the book are invited to contact the relevant author.

Thomas Handler
October 1996

Contents

		Page
The Editor		v
Baker & McKenzie		v
Preface		vii
1	Environmental Regulation of the European Community	1
	Joachim Scherer, Baker & McKenzie, Frankfurt	
	EC Environmental law and the internal market	1
	Treaty rules – Single European Act – Maastricht Treaty	2
	Jurisprudence of the European Court of Justice	3
	Legislative and other instruments	5
	Air pollution	5
	Water pollution	9
	Waste management	13
	Noise pollution	19
	Regulation of hazardous substances	20
	Biotechnology	21
	General environmental measures	21
2	Environmental Regulation in Belgium	27
	Paul Herten, Baker & McKenzie, Brussels	
	Sources of environmental regulation	27
	Specific laws and regulations applicable to certain areas of environmental regulation	30
	Environmental permitting schemes	32
	Enforcement of environmental regulations	33
	Environmental initiatives	34
3	Environmental Regulation in the Czech Republic	37
	Marek J. Svoboda, Baker & McKenzie, Prague	
	Introduction	37
	Sources of environmental regulation	38

Specific provisions applicable to certain areas of
   environmental regulation   39
Enforcement of environmental regulations   43
Government environmental policy   45

4 Environmental Regulation in Egypt   47
   Samir M. Hamza, Baker & McKenzie, Cairo
   Sources of environmental regulation   47
   Specific provisions, laws, executive regulations and
     presidential decrees applicable to certain areas of
     environmental regulation   48
   The Agency for Environmental Affairs   53
   Administrative and judicial procedures under the law   53

5 Environmental Regulation in England and Wales   55
   Thomas Handler, Baker & McKenzie, London
   Sources of environmental regulation   55
   Specific provisions, statutes and regulations applicable
     to certain areas of environmental regulation   57
   Environmental permitting schemes   65
   Enforcement of environmental regulations   67
   Freedom of access by the public to information on the
     environment   70
   Environmental management   71
   Economic instruments   72
   Major environmental initiatives and pending proposals   72

6 Environmental Regulation in France   75
   Alex Dowding, Baker & McKenzie, Paris
   Sources of environmental regulation   75
   Specific provisions constituting environmental
     regulation   76
   Environmental permitting schemes   81
   Enforcement of environmental regulation   82
   Availability of information on the environment   86
   Environmental trends   86

Contents

7 Environmental Regulation in the Federal Republic of
   Germany   89
   Joachim Scherer, Baker & McKenzie, Frankfurt/Main
   Regulatory and organisational framework   89
   Sources of environmental regulation   89
   Specific provisions, statutes and regulations applicable
      to certain areas of environmental regulation   91
   Liability for historic contamination: the "Altlasten"
      problem   101
   Hazardous substances   104
   Enforcement of environmental regulation   107
   Assessing and allocating environmental liability   109
   Major environmental initiatives   111

8 Environmental Regulation in Hungary   113
   Gabriella Kicska, Baker & McKenzie, Budapest
   Sources of environmental regulation   113
   Specific provisions applicable to certain areas of
      environmental regulation   118
   Procedures; time periods   123

9 Environmental Regulation in Italy   125
   Pierfrancesco Federici and Angelo Guido Galeotti,
      Baker & McKenzie, Milan
   Sources of environmental regulation   125
   Specific provisions, statutes and regulations applicable
      to certain areas of environmental regulation   126
   Environmental permitting schemes   132
   National agency for environmental protection   133

10 Environmental Regulation in the Republic of Kazakstan 135
   Tamara Barnes, Baker & McKenzie, Almaty
   Sources of environmental regulation   135
   Environmental payments   136
   Liability for past environmental damage   140
   State regulation   141
   Major environmental initiatives   141
   Conclusion   141

11 Environmental Regulation in the Netherlands   143
    Hans V. van Ophem, Baker & McKenzie, Amsterdam
    Sources of environmental regulation   143
    Specific provisions, statutes and regulations applicable
        to certain areas of environmental regulation   145
    Environmental permitting schemes   149
    Enforcement of environmental regulation   151
    Major environmental initiatives   153
    Products and the environment   156

12 Environmental Regulation in Poland   157
    Jur Grusczyńsky and Waleria Skarżyńska, Baker &
        McKenzie, Warsaw
    Sources of environmental regulation   157
    Specific provisions, statutes and regulations applicable
        to certain areas of environmental regulation   158
    Environmental permitting schemes   161
    Enforcement of environmental regulation   163
    Economic indicators   164
    Major environmental initiatives and pending proposals 165

13 Environmental Regulation in the Russian Federation 167
    Jean A. Brough, Baker & McKenzie, Moscow
    Sources of environmental regulation   167
    Specific provisions, statutes and regulations applicable
        to certain areas of environmental regulation   169
    Environmental permitting schemes   172
    Environmental insurance and state environmental
        appraisal   172
    Enforcement of environmental regulation   173
    Other matters affecting the environment   176

14 Environmental Regulation in Spain   177
    Xavier Junquera and Eusebio Pujol, Baker & McKenzie,
        Barcelona
    Sources of environmental regulation   177
    Specific legislation and regulations applicable to certain
        areas of environmental regulation   180
    Environmental permitting schemes   196

Contents

Enforcement of environmental regulation 197
Recent developments and major current initiatives 199

15 Environmental Regulation in Sweden 201
Bengt Bergendal and Johan Norman, Baker & McKenzie, Stockholm
Sources of environmental regulation 201
Specific provisions, statutes and regulations applicable to certain areas of environmental regulation 204
Environmental permitting schemes 205
Enforcement of environmental regulation 207
Major environmental initiatives 208

16 Environmental Regulation in Switzerland 209
Daniel Peregrina, Baker & McKenzie, Geneva
Sources of environmental regulation 209
Specific provisions, statutes and regulations applicable to certain areas of environmental regulation 210
Environmental permitting schemes 215
Enforcement of environmental regulation 216
Major environmental initiatives and proposals 218

Index 221

Chapter 1
Environmental Regulation of the European Community

Joachim Scherer*
Baker & McKenzie, Frankfurt

EC Environmental Law and the Internal Market

The potential economic and social benefits of the European Community's (EC) single market have an environmental dimension. Without suitable development of environmental policies and legislation, the economic growth which is expected as a consequence of the internal market may have a considerable impact on environmental quality.

The ecological necessity of an EC environmental policy has long been recognised in the various environmental action programmes submitted by the EC Commission and adopted by the Council. Since the Council adopted the First Action Programme on the Environment in 1973, the EC has adopted numerous measures and some 300 legislative acts on the environment. Many legislative acts concern water pollution, but legislation on air pollution, hazardous substances, waste management and incentives has become increasingly important.

In the light of the programme to complete the internal market, the Commission has increased its activities in the environmental field. In December 1992 the Council adopted a resolution on the EC Fifth Action Programme on the Environment, which sets out

*The author gratefully acknowledges the assistance of Grace Nacimiento (Baker & McKenzie, Frankfurt) in the preparation of this chapter.

1

the Commission's priorities in the field of environmental policy from 1993 to 2000. The action programme stresses the necessity for a change of strategy to achieve sustainable development. Particular emphasis is placed on voluntary participation by industry to consolidate the mainly legislative approach of the EC to environmental protection, the development of adequate economic instruments in the context of environmental protection and the need to develop environmental technologies.

Treaty Rules – Single European Act – Maastricht Treaty

The 1957 Treaty of Rome did not specifically refer to the need for an environmental policy but, given the necessity for one, the EC began developing a policy in the early 1970s. This development was supported by the European Court of Justice (ECJ), which declared that the protection of the environment was one of the essential objectives of the EC.

The Single European Act 1987 (SEA) was a very important development because it confirmed the ability of the EC to legislate in the environmental area and laid down specific powers to act. The SEA lays down objectives for EC actions relating to the environment, namely:

- to preserve, protect and improve the quality of the environment;
- to contribute to the protection of human health; and
- to ensure prudent and rational utilisation of natural resources.

The three basic principles of EC environmental law and policy as laid down in the SEA are:

- preventive action should be taken;
- environmental damage should as a priority be rectified at source; and
- the polluter should pay.

The SEA lists factors to be taken into account in deciding on steps in this field. It also adds that the EC shall take action to the extent that the environmental policy objectives can be attained better at an

EC level than at the level of individual member states. Moreover, the SEA gives member states the right to maintain or introduce more stringent protective measures "compatible with this Treaty".

The Treaty on European Union, commonly referred to as the Maastricht Treaty, entered into force on 1 November 1993. After the entry into force of the Maastricht Treaty, some confusion emerged over the correct use of the terms "European Union" and "European Community". While the Council has renamed itself the "Council of the European Union", the Commission has retained its name "Commission of the European Communities". Since the term "European Union" is not defined in the Maastricht Treaty and is still subject to controversy, for present purposes the term "European Community" is maintained.

The Maastricht Treaty lists environmental protection as one of the basic objectives of the EC. Article 130r of the EC Treaty lists the goals of environmental policy, establishes guidelines for protection measures and sets out the principle of cooperation between the EC and the member states. The goals of environmental policy correspond to the goals already set out in the SEA and add the promotion of international measures for the solution of regional or global environmental problems. Furthermore, Article 130r of the EC Treaty establishes the following guidelines for the development of European environmental policy: the available scientific technical data, the environmental conditions in individual regions of the Community, the advantages and disadvantages of actions, the economic and social development of the EC and the balanced development of its regions. The Maastricht Treaty establishes the cooperation procedure (Art. 189c) as the general rule for legislative decision-making in the environmental field, subject however to several broad exceptions. Thus, unanimity continues to be required for all provisions "primarily of a fiscal nature" (including the proposed tax on energy use).

Jurisprudence of the European Court of Justice

In 1989 the ECJ stated, in a case brought by the Commission against Denmark, that protection of the environment is a legitimate justification for national rules which have the effect of impeding the free movement of goods within the Community (and thereby infringing Art. 30 of the EC Treaty). It remains to be seen whether the ECJ will apply this principle to national environmental measures laying down stricter standards than harmonising EC legislation.

The ECJ has delineated the EC's legislative powers in the environmental field under Arts. 100a and 130s of the EC Treaty by holding that the directive on pollution caused by titanium dioxide was invalid because it had been adopted on the basis of Art. 130s. The ECJ found that the directive represented not only an environmental measure but also a harmonising measure for the establishment of the internal market. The ECJ pointed out that EC legislation which serves this dual purpose must be based on Art. 100a, because this provision ensures a higher degree of participation by the European Parliament than Art. 130s and provides for majority vote in the Council rather than unanimity.

In a ruling on the framework directive on waste, the ECJ held that the Council had correctly chosen Art. 130s of the EC Treaty rather than Art. 100a as the legal basis for the directive. Contrary to the Commission's view, the ECJ stated that the mere fact that a legislative act affects the creation or operation of the internal market does not in itself justify the use of Art. 100a and that Art. 100a was not the appropriate legal basis when legislation had harmonisation of conditions of the internal market only as a secondary effect.

In a 1996 ruling on a 1994 annexe to Directive 91/414 on the marketing of pesticides, the ECJ held that the annexe violated the spirit of the basic Directive 91/414 by modifying the scope of obligations imposed on the member states in the directive. The European Parliament had attacked the annexe, claiming that, since it modified the basic directive, the Parliament should have been consulted by the Commission under the legislative procedure established in the EC Treaty. The ECJ confirmed that the modification of Directive 91/414 considerably reduced the protection provided for groundwater as established in the original directive and that therefore the Parliament was justified in its claim. This ruling is thought to have strengthened the Parliament's rights of participation in the legislative process.

Legislative and other Instruments

In practice, the most common instrument used by both the Council and the Commission is the directive, which requires implementation by national legislation. Since member states have repeatedly failed to meet the deadlines of implementing directives, the Commission is trying to improve the monitoring of implementation. To this end, the Council adopted in December 1991 a directive standardising and rationalising reports on the implementation of directives relating to the environment.

Furthermore, the Commission started utilising recommendations in conjunction with "voluntary agreements" between the Commission and specific sectors of industry as new tools of environmental policy. The Fifth Action Programme indicates that the Commission intends to use a range of legal and non-legal instruments in order to promote a genuine interaction between the main parties involved, including governments and companies, as well as economic sectors such as industry, energy, transport and tourism.

Air Pollution

EC legislation on air pollution is much less comprehensive than legislation on the aquatic environment. The legislation takes, in essence, three regulatory approaches: the setting of air quality objectives; control of source-oriented emissions. *e.g.* automotive emissions and emissions from stationary sources; and control of emissions, *e.g.* specific substances.

In order to combat the greenhouse effect, the Council in December 1992 amended the regulation on substances that deplete the ozone layer and thus speed up the phasing out of such substances. For instance, the production of CFCs and carbon tetrachloride were required to be phased out by the end of 1994. Following the Council's authorisation of the Commission to negotiate adaptions and changes to the Montreal Protocol, the Commission proposed in June 1993 a regulation for the elimination of HCFs by 2014 and a reduction by 50% in 1999 of methyl bromide. After the Seventh Conference on the Montreal Protocol, the Council of Environment Ministers in March 1996 adopted conclusions evaluating the results of the conference and, based on this evaluation, asked for stricter provisions for the prohibition of HCF in the 1993 proposed regulation.

In September 1992 the Council adopted a directive on air pollution by ozone, which provides for harmonised procedures for monitoring, exchange of information and warning of the population if certain thresholds of ozone concentration are exceeded. In 1994 the Commission submitted a proposal for a framework directive on the assessment and control of ambient air quality. The proposal establishes a system allowing the EC to determine limit values for emissions through future individual measures, thereby replacing the existing directives.

With regard to CO_2 emissions, the Council decided in 1990 to stabilise CO_2 emissions by the year 2000 at 1990 levels. The EC's strategy to limit carbon dioxide emissions and to improve energy efficiency includes a tax on such emissions and on energy use. The Commission's proposal for a directive introducing a tax on CO_2 emissions and energy made in May 1992, eventually failed. The Commission adopted a new proposal in 1995 which bases the taxes on the volume of CO_2 emitted as well as the energy content of the substance from which the emissions came. The proposal leaves it to the member states to determine the tax rates by the year 2000, taking into consideration the objective of reducing CO_2 emissions. After this has been done, the Commission plans to introduce a harmonised CO_2/energy tax.

The EC has acceded to the UN Convention on climate change and to other important international conventions, such as the Geneva Agreement on Long-range Transboundary Air Pollution of 1979 and the Protocol thereto of 1993 on the control of emissions of nitrogen oxides.

Air Quality

Among the most important EC measures on air pollution is Directive 80/779 on limit values for sulphur dioxide and suspended particulates. Following the Dutch regulatory approach, this directive fixes mandatory ambient air quality standards and stricter non-binding guide values for sulphur dioxide and suspended particulates in the atmosphere. Stricter standards were introduced in 1989. The directive specifies measurement methods and establishes three types of zones in which air quality standards for sulphur dioxide and particulates may differ from the general standards. In principle, member states were obliged to take the necessary steps to ensure that the mandatory standards were achieved by 1983. A more far-reaching proposal of the Commission for the reduction of sulphur dioxide according to the Geneva Agreement 1979 has not yet been adopted. A similar regulatory approach was adopted by the directive for air quality standards for nitrogen oxide, requiring compliance by 31 December 1993.

Emissions from Motor Vehicles

The 1970 directive on air pollution by motor vehicles, as amended, lays down emission standards for carbon monoxide, hydrocarbons and nitrogen oxides together with specific testing methods. These emission values have gradually become stricter. Differentiated emission values have been established on the basis of Directive 88/76, which distinguishes between small cars (below 1.4 litres), medium-sized cars (between 1.4 and 2 litres) and large cars (over 2 litres).

In June 1991 the Council agreed on a directive to bring the standards for motor vehicles up to 2.5 tonnes into line. The directive introduces limit values similar to US standards from 1 July 1992 which typically can only be met with computer-controlled catalytic converters.

In June 1993 the Council adopted a directive on air pollution by motor vehicles above 2.5 tonnes and light utility vehicles which adjusted the limit values for these vehicles to the strict limit values for vehicles up to 2.5 tonnes, thus making the EC emission standards the lowest in the world. In 1994 even stricter values were adopted for motor vehicles under 2.5 tonnes. Adjustment for the heavier vehicles is expected in the near future.

In June 1996, the Commission adopted a draft directive setting new maximum limits for vehicle emissions from the year 2000 on. This draft directive on emissions from road transport provides for a reduction in the limit values of exhaust emissions in two stages: 20%–40% reduction in various pollutants, such as CO, HC, NO_x particles for diesel, applicable to all new vehicles from 2001 and stricter limit values for 2005 which should be set by the end of 1996, taking account of the latest technological developments.

Also in June 1996 the Commission adopted a draft directive on fuel quality (petrol and diesel). The draft directive provides for harmonized limit values to be applied in 2000 and for different parameters of lead-free petrol and diesel fuel, *e.g.* benzene and sulphur, with proven effect on emissions. The draft directive also aims at a gradual elimination of leaded petrol by 2000 and the creation of a uniform system monitoring the quality of fuel distributed on the market.

Agreement has not yet been reached on the proposal for a directive on excise duties on motor fuels from agricultural sources ("bio-fuels"), which aims to make bio-fuels competitive with fossil fuels.

Emissions from Industrial Plants

The 1984 directive on combating air pollution from industrial plants marked yet another shift in strategy in air pollution control. The purpose of this framework directive is to reduce and prevent air pollution from industrial plants, in particular in the following sectors: the energy industry, production and processing of metals, manufacture of non-metallic mineral products, the chemical industry, waste disposal and major pulp-paper manufacturers.

On the basis of the 1984 framework directive, the Council adopted mandatory emission limit values for certain emissions from municipal waste incineration plants which had to be implemented by December 1990. The Council has reached a political agreement on the proposed directive on the incineration of hazardous waste, determining the conditions under which incineration plants may be operated and setting limit values for emissions based on the concept of best available technology. This directive contains a new approach in that it not only covers air pollution but also protection of soil and water. It will apply to any solid or liquid waste as defined in the 1991 framework directive except for flammable liquid waste, certain hazardous wastes resulting from research, municipal waste and sewage sludge originating in urban waste waters.

After more than five years of controversy, the Large Combustion Plants Directive was adopted in June 1988. It obliges member states to establish programmes for the reduction of sulphur dioxide and nitrogen dioxide emissions by three steps up to the year 2003. In 1994, the Council adopted a common position on proposed amendments to the directive. The common position extends the SO_2 limit values to new plants with a capacity between 50 and 100 MW.

Specific Substances

Further directives provide for the gradual reduction and ultimate elimination of lead in petrol, the establishment of a distribution system for unleaded petrol and limit values for lead in the air to protect human beings against the effects of lead in the environment.

The 1987 directive on the prevention and reduction of environmental pollution by asbestos obliges member states to take the necessary measures to prevent asbestos emissions into the air, asbestos discharges into the aquatic environment and solid asbestos waste as far as reasonably practicable.

In June 1993 the Council adopted a directive on the sulphur content in gas oils. It establishes limit values for diesel fuels (0.2% by weight from 1 October 1994 and 0.05% by weight from 1 October 1996) and other gas oils (0.2% by weight from 1 October 1994).

Water Pollution

The prevention and cure of water pollution is one of the priority areas in EC environmental policy and it is in this sector that the EC has the most comprehensive legislation. Three different regulatory strategies are being pursued: water quality standards;

effluent standards for dangerous substances and specific products; and prevention of marine pollution.

These strategies are complemented by monitoring and information exchange requirements.

The Commission has issued a communication which suggests an outline proposal for a general Water Resources Framework Directive. By replacing six other measures this directive could improve the coherence of member states' legislation on water. However, environmental groups have expressed their concern that member states could regain some authority to set specific water quality standards on the basis of a general directive and that such standards would be less strict than EC standards.

Water Quality Standards

In order to reduce and prevent water pollution, the Council has adopted numerous directives establishing a system of water quality objectives and standards for certain types of surface waters classified according to their use: drinking water, bathing water and water for harvesting fish and shellfish.

Whilst the directives lay down criteria to determine the use of particular waters, the final decision on classification is left to the member states. The structure of the various directives follows a certain pattern. Depending upon the type of use (drinking water, bathing water, etc.), the directives establish maximum allowable concentration (MAC) and guide levels (GL) within certain parameters. In order to ensure quality control measures, the directives establish methods of measuring and the frequency for sampling and analysis.

To date, the Council has adopted five directives which establish quality standards for surface waters, the most important of which is Directive 75/440. It establishes three categories of quality standards for surface water intended for drinking water, as well as stricter quality goals or "guidelines" and standard methods for water treatment. While this directive is not applicable to groundwater, a Council recommendation advises that the directive should also be used for the abstraction of drinking water from groundwater. Surface water which does not conform to the least stringent of the mandatory standards may, in principle, not be used as drinking water. Measuring methods are laid down in part by the directive itself and in part by a special directive adopted in 1979.

Additional water quality standards are established by Directive 80/778 on the quality of water intended for human consumption. This directive establishes maximum allowable concentration and guide levels for water which is intended for human consumption, either in its original state or after treatment, regardless of origin and whether supplied for consumption or used in the production of products intended for human consumption. In 1995 the Commission presented a proposal for a directive concerning the quality of water intended for human consumption which provides for stricter limit values.

The Bathing Water Directive 76/160 is intended to reduce the pollution of bathing water and to protect water against further deterioration. It applies to all running and still fresh water and sea water which is designated for bathing use. The directive lays down mandatory quality standards and stricter quality guidelines, while leaving the designation of bathing areas to the member states.

Finally, two directives lay down quality standards for the protection of aquatic life: the Fish Water Directive 78/659 and the Shellfish Water Directive 79/923.

Effluent Standards for Hazardous Substances and Specific Products

One of the cornerstones of EC environmental legislation on water pollution is Directive 76/464 on pollution caused by certain dangerous substances discharged into the aquatic environment, as amended in July 1990.

The purpose of the Aquatic Environment Directive is to eliminate, over a defined period of time, water pollution caused by the discharge of particularly dangerous substances into water and to reduce water pollution by the discharge of other less hazardous substances. The directive applies to inland surface and internal coastal waters. It is complemented by Directive 80/68 on groundwater which follows the same regulatory pattern but contains even stricter standards.

The Aquatic Environment Directive sets out two lists of hazardous substances: the black list and the grey list. Pollution from substances listed in the black list must be "eliminated" by means of a system of uniform effluent standards. This list, which includes mercury, cadmium, persistent organic chemicals, carcinogenic substances and non-biodegradable oils, is not exhaustive but requires further specification.

Additional specific directives have been adopted on specific substances, for instance on the discharge of mercury, cadmium, hexachlorocyclohexane and nitrates from the farming industry. A 1985 proposal on the discharge of chromium was withdrawn by the Commission in 1993.

Member states must establish implementation programmes for reduction of water pollution by grey list substances. These programmes must contain water quality standards which may, however, to a large extent be determined by the member states.

In May 1991 the Council adopted a far reaching directive on urban waste water treatment. This directive obliges the member states, amongst other things, to introduce biological waste water treatment installations for all discharges from agglomerations of more than 15,000 inhabitants by December 2000 and for discharges to fresh water and estuaries from agglomerations of between 2,000 and 10,000 inhabitants by December 2005.

A product-orientated approach has been chosen by Directive 73/404 on detergents, which prohibits the marketing and the use of detergents with an average level of bio-degradability of the surfactants below 90%. Additional directives lay down the methods to be used in testing bio-degradability.

Prevention of Marine Pollution

In order to prevent accidental pollution, two directives concerning the pilotage of vessels in the North Sea and the English Channel have been issued. These directives set out minimum safety requirements for domestic and certain foreign tankers entering or leaving EC ports. In a resolution of June 1990, the Council requested member states to strengthen the control of foreign vessels in port.

The Commission has also proposed minimum requirements for vessels entering or leaving EC ports carrying packages of

12

dangerous or polluting goods, in order to minimise the risk of accidents which might damage the marine environment.

The Commission's proposal for a directive prohibiting the dumping of waste at sea is still awaiting approval. Progress in this field was made in March 1990 by the Third North Sea Conference, which adopted a declaration confirming the objectives already defined during the second conference in 1978 and defined new ones. The Commission proposes to transform these objectives into binding EC law in order to achieve reduction of the dumping of non-bio-degradables and to improve nitrate and phosphorous management.

In the wake of the La Coruna and Shetland Islands oil spills, the Council of Ministers agreed to establish an EC policy on safety at sea and has asked the Commission to present proposals for measures. These proposals will focus on the application of safety standards set up for certain vessels by the International Maritime Organisation, a directive on information requirements *vis-à-vis* EC authorities where passing through EC waters, the setting of criteria for the inspection and detention of dangerous vessels, as well as the establishment of exclusion zones in ecologically sensitive areas.

Waste Management

Waste management policy will remain one of the EC's major priorities.

In a policy paper adopted in 1989, the Commission set out "A Community Strategy for Waste Management", reiterating the main objectives of the EC's waste management policy up to the year 2000: waste prevention by technology and by product; waste recycling and re-use; optimising final disposal; regulation of transport; and remedial action. This policy paper was endorsed by the Council in May 1990.

Framework Directive on Waste

The 1975 framework directive established basic obligations for the member states to encourage the prevention, recycling and processing of waste and to ensure that waste is disposed of without injury to health and the environment. Member states were obliged to establish waste disposal plans and permit systems for businesses involved in commercial treatment, storing or dumping of waste and to prevent uncontrolled waste disposal.

This directive was amended by Directive 91/156, adopted in March 1991. Under the new regime, which had to be implemented by member states by 1 April 1993, "waste" is defined in terms of specific categories of substances which the holder discards or is required to discard. The directive obliges the member states to give preference to the prevention or reduction of waste production and to the recovery of waste by means of recycling, reuse or reclamation and by the use of waste as a source of energy. In January 1994 the Commission published the European Waste Index, specifying the waste categories covered by the directive. However, because of a lack of precision of the index, its binding effect is disputed.

Toxic and Dangerous Waste

A number of directives cover waste containing particularly dangerous substances.

The Hazardous Waste Directive 78/319 governs waste requiring special treatment in view of the risks it presents to health or the environment, including arsenic, heavy metals, pesticides, chlorinated solvents, pharmaceutical compounds and asbestos. The directive followed the same regulatory approach as the framework directive (permit requirement for the storage, treatment or dumping of toxic and dangerous waste, application of the polluter pays principle and establishment of waste disposal plans, etc.).

In December 1991 the Council adopted Directive 91/689, replacing Directive 78/319 with effect from June 1995. The new directive is in essence similar to Directive 78/319, but lays down more stringent requirements for the control and supervision of hazardous waste. It contains more precise definitions, including detailed annexes with lists of groups and types of hazardous waste. Categories of hazardous waste are further specified in the 1994 Index of Hazardous Wastes. Member states must ensure that any discharge of hazardous waste is recorded and identified and must take measures to prohibit the mixing of hazardous waste with other waste, unless it is a necessary part of waste treatment. Member states must submit to the Commission information on any installation or undertaking which carries out recovery or disposal of hazardous waste.

Specific regulatory regimes have been established, *inter alia*, for the disposal of waste oils, PCBs, waste from the titanium dioxide industry, and batteries and accumulators containing dangerous substances. The Titanium Dioxide Directive has been complemented by a directive which prohibits the dumping on land and into water of any solid waste, strong acid waste, treatment waste, weak acid waste or neutralised waste.

Prevention and Recycling of Waste

The EC has enacted only one directive applying the principle of re-use and recycling. The 1975 directive on waste from containers of liquids for human consumption merely obliged member states to adopt programmes for the achievement of the goals set out in the directive in order to reduce the quantities of beverage container waste; the directive did not oblige member states to implement specific measures for the recycling or recovery of such waste.

In 1994, the EC adopted Directive 94/62 on packaging and packaging waste. The directive is aimed at decreasing trade barriers within the internal market and reducing the impact of packaging waste on the environment. To this end, the existing national provisions are to be harmonised, the amount of packaging waste reduced, and recycling for necessary packaging promoted.

The directive establishes a hierarchy of waste policy measures; first prevention, then recycling and eventually incineration.

Member states are obliged by 30 June 2001 to recycle between 50% and 60% by weight of packaging waste and between 25% and 45% by weight of packaging material contained in packaging waste. By 30 June 2006 the Council will decide on substantially higher quotas. Member states who have already established higher quotas are allowed to maintain them if they serve environmental protection purposes and avoid distortions on the internal market.

The directive provides for a number of measures to be taken by the member states in order to achieve the recycling quotas. Member states must establish take-back, collection and recycling systems. After implementation of the directive, packaging material must conform to certain requirements for production, composition and recyclability. Member states must inform the public, in particular users of packaging, about the possibilities of recycling. The Council will decide within two years on the labelling of packaging.

Transfrontier Shipment of Waste

The 1984 directive on transfrontier shipment of toxic and dangerous waste made such shipment subject to strict record-keeping requirements. Toxic and dangerous waste transported in the course of disposal had to be accompanied by an identification form containing information on its nature, composition, volume, the name and address of the waste producer and of the person taking delivery of the waste and the location of the site of final disposal. The regulatory system was based on authorisations issued by the importing country; the exporting country could object, but only on the basis of an existing waste disposal plan.

Since many member states failed to implement this 1984 directive, in February 1993 the Council adopted a regulation concerning shipments of waste into, within and from the Community. As a legal basis, the Council chose Art. 130s instead of Art. 100a, thus depriving the European Parliament of a second reading in the legislative process, and the Parliament challenged the regulation before the ECJ. However, in a ruling of 1994, the Court confirmed Art. 130s as appropriate.

Under the regulation any transfer of waste for disposal between member states is subject to a notification procedure by way of consignment notes indicating the origin, type, quantity and destination of the waste, including the names of the waste generator and of the recipient. The notifications must be sent to the respective competent authorities in the states of origin and of destination. A similar system applies to transfers of waste for recycling.

The regulation restricts any transport of waste for disposal to

EC member states and EFTA member states that are also parties to the Basle Convention on the Control of Transboundary Movements of Hazardous Wastes and their Disposal. As for wastes for recycling, any export to non-OECD states and states not party to the Basle Convention is prohibited. Member states may take measures generally or partially prohibiting shipments of waste, provided they are in accordance with the EC Treaty. The principle of self-sufficiency in waste disposal has thus been given priority. In order to alleviate concerns over restrictions on the free movement of goods, the regulation incorporates a declaration by the Council and the Commission that prohibiting measures must be implemented in a "spirit of cooperation". The regulation took effect in May 1994 and implements the Basle Convention, which the Council had decided in February 1993 to ratify.

As for waste incineration installations, a directive on the incineration of hazardous waste was adopted in 1994 and it must be implemented by the member states by the end of 1996. The directive provides for permit requirements for new incineration installations and prescribes incineration temperatures, emission values and requirements for the discharge of waste water. The directive will apply to existing incineration installations from June 2000.

In response to the nuclear waste scandals of 1988, the Commission adopted in 1992 a directive on the supervision and control of shipments establishing an EC notification, inspection and control system for radioactive waste movements within, between, into and out of member states. The directive was to be implemented by the member states by 1 January 1995.

Waste Disposal Installations

A proposal for a directive on the landfill of waste which was submitted by the Commission in March 1992 has now been withdrawn by the Commission. In 1994 the Council had adopted a common position on the draft directive, amending the text significantly. In May 1996 the Parliament voted on the common position and rejected it. The Commission subsequently decided to withdraw the proposal. However, the proposal may be revived later in

1996. The proposed directive was intended to supplement the provisions concerning waste disposal installations in the 1975 and 1991 framework directives and to flesh out the general requirements in these directives for safe waste disposal. The proposed directive set out extensive security and control measures to be adopted by the member states over waste to be disposed of in landfills. There were detailed provisions for categories of waste, acceptance procedures, control and closure procedures, as well as a liability provision concerning the operator of disposal sites. The annexes laid down specific technical standards to be applied for the determination of categories of waste and the requirements for their treatment. In an amended proposal, the Commission called for a ban on mixtures of different types of waste in the same site, although this co-disposal system is used in all member states. The proposed phasing out of the co-disposal system and its eventual ban led to substantial dispute and eventually to the failure of the proposal.

Civil Liability for Damage Caused by Waste

Following discussion in the European Parliament, the Commission submitted in June 1991 an amended proposal for a directive on civil liability for environmental damage or injury caused by waste. The proposal was structured similarly to the 1985 Product Liability Directive and is based upon two principles embodied in the SEA: preventive action and the polluter pays.

The proposal applies to all waste generated in the course of commercial activities, except nuclear waste and pollution from certain hydrocarbons; domestic waste is also excluded. The proposal imposes unlimited and strict ("no-fault") liability on the producer of the waste, but it does not prevent a waste producer from seeking compensation from third parties (*e.g.* the waste transporter) if the damage was caused by their negligence. If the producer cannot be identified, holders or (where the waste was transferred to an authorised disposal plant) the disposer will be liable. An importer into the EC of waste is considered a producer. If several parties (*e.g.* producers of different wastes, handlers of the same waste in a chain leading from waste producer to waste disposer) are liable, they will all be held jointly and severally liable.

Liability arises for damage to persons (death or injury) and "significant impairment" of the environment caused by waste. "Impairment" is defined as a significant physical, chemical or biological deterioration of the environment. Member states must adopt laws determining the potential plaintiff (which must include common interest environmental groups), the remedies available for the reinstatement of the environment, and the reimbursement of reinstatement costs.

No liability arises if the damage or impairment of the environment was caused by an intentional act of a third party or resulted from *force majeure*. The holding of a permit issued by a public authority does not in itself relieve the producer of liability.

The directive is not to apply to damage or impairment caused by an incident before the date the directive is adopted; however, because "incident" is not defined, retroactivity cannot be ruled out.

The proposal requires compulsory insurance by producers and disposers of waste and envisages further provisions, including a European fund, to cover uncompensated loss.

This proposal, if adopted, would be the first EC instrument providing for liability for environmental damage. It is the first step by the Commission towards a more comprehensive system of strict liability for environmental damage. The proposal has not progressed in light of consideration of the Green Paper on Remedying Environmental Damage (see below).

Noise Pollution

Community legislation on noise pollution is primarily focused on limiting noise from vehicles. The regulatory approach is in general based on common product standards rather than mandatory noise levels. The directives concern noise generated by, among other products, motor vehicles, machinery such as electric generators, power cranes, compressors and lawn mowers, and noise emitted from construction machinery and equipment.

Directive 89/629 concerns the limitation of noise emissions from civil subsonic jets. In March 1992 the Council adopted a directive limiting the use of the noisiest of jet aircraft. This means that the "chapter 2 aircraft" under the annexe to the Chicago Convention will be gradually eliminated by 1 April 2002.

The Council has adopted a directive reducing maximum vehicle noise emissions by 50% from October 1996. Member states will be required to ban new vehicles emitting noise exceeding specified levels.

Regulation of Hazardous Substances

The EC regulatory framework comprises:

- a system of classification, packaging and labelling of chemicals;
- pre-market control of chemicals;
- restrictions on the marketing and use of certain substances; and
- rules on the storage of hazardous substances and on the major accident hazards of industrial activities in conjunction with hazardous substances.

In April 1993 the Council adopted a regulation on the evaluation and control of risks presented by existing chemical substances to human beings and the environment. The regulation provides for risk assessments of the substances listed in the European Inventory of Existing Commercial Substances (EINECS).

The transfrontier movement of hazardous substances is governed by a regulation on exports and imports of dangerous chemicals. The exporter of dangerous chemicals listed in the regulation is obliged to receive prior informed consent from any importing country outside the EC.

Following the dioxin accident in Seveso in 1976, Directive 82/501 on the hazards of major accidents in certain industry activities was adopted. The directive applies to approximately 2000 industrial installations in the EC. In reaction to the Sandoz accident in Basle in 1986, the scope of application was extended to the storage of hazardous substances and preparations. In 1995 the Commission prepared a proposed amendment to the Seveso Directive which is based on the concept of self and public monitoring by requiring, for example, publicly accessible safety reports. The EC is participating in the preparation of a draft International Agreement on the Prevention of Industrial Accidents which contains provisions similar to those contained in the Seveso Directive.

Biotechnology

The Council has indicated six priority areas for EC activity. These include the regulation of the biotechnology sector, intellectual property rights, research and development and demonstration projects. Two directives on biotechnology were adopted in April 1990. The first, on the deliberate release of genetically modified organisms into the environment, provides for notification and case-by-case approval. The second covers the laboratory use of genetically modified micro-organisms. The Commission aims in the future at the simplification of the notification and approval procedures established in the two directives in order to promote the European biotechnology industry.

General Environmental Measures

In addition to sector-specific legislation, the Commission is in the process of establishing a comprehensive framework of procedural and organisational rules in the field of environmental policy.

European Environment Agency

In May 1990 the Council adopted a regulation on the establishment of the European Environment Agency, in which third countries may also participate. The regulation came into effect in 1993 after the agency's seat had been established in Copenhagen. For the first two years of its operation the agency is merely to record, collate and assess data, and then its powers will be reviewed and possibly extended.

European Environmental Forum

In 1993 the Commission established a European Environmental Forum with general consulting functions. The Forum has 32 members, elected from the economic and environmental protection sectors.

Environmental Information

In a major step towards more transparency of administrative behaviour in the environmental field, a directive on the freedom of access to environmental information was adopted in June 1990. The directive provides a general right of access to information about the environment which is in the possession of a public authority. This right may be restricted, however, in order to prevent the disclosure of business secrets. Member states who failed to implement the directive by the end of 1992 have to face the consequences of the possibility that the directive may have direct effect.

Environmental Effects – Eco-Audits

Following the 1985 directive on environmental impact assessment, which establishes a system for the assessment of the environmental compatibility of certain public and private projects, the Commission decided in an internal communication to apply the environmental impact assessment to EC projects and legislation. The Commission adopted a proposal for the amendment of the directive in 1993 which aims at a clearer definition of the projects covered as well as at a more harmonised implementation of the directive. In particular, the proposed amendments add nuclear and chemical plants to the list of projects for which an impact study is compulsory. The Council of Environment Ministers reached political agreement in 1995 on a common position on the proposed amendments.

In June 1993 the Council adopted a regulation on an environmental management and auditing scheme for European industry.

The regulation establishes a voluntary system for the evaluation and improvement of the environmental performance of industrial activities at certain sites. This "eco-management and audit scheme" also provides for the supply of information to the public on the results of the environmental audits carried out by independent verifiers. Environmental performance should be constantly improved by the economically viable use of "the best technologies available".

Eco-Label

In March 1992, the Council adopted a regulation establishing an EC system of "eco-labelling". It provides for a "European eco-logical label" (a flower made up of 12 stars and an "E" for "Europe") which can be affixed to products meeting certain environmental standards. The regulation is concerned with the total impact of the product, from production through distribution, use or consumption and disposal. A product will only be permitted to bear the label if it is substantially less damaging to the environment than other products of the same category. The label will be awarded on the basis of detailed ecological criteria to be adopted for each product category. They include the raw materials used, the means of production, the dimension and packaging of the product and its disposal. In May 1993, the Commission set up guidelines for the costs and fees involved. In 1994, a model contract for the award of the eco-label was published. The Commission has adopted environmental criteria for granting the eco-label to paints and varnishes, washing machines, dishwashers, soil improvers, toilet paper, kitchen rolls, laundry detergents and single-ended light bulbs.

Environmental Liability

The Commission is considering the possibility of introducing a new scheme of liability for environmental damage. One objective of this scheme would be to introduce the obligation to restore environmental damage whenever such restoration was feasible.

Furthermore, the Commission is considering harmonisation of member state laws on liability for environmental damage and establishment of joint compensation mechanisms to cover costs of environmental restoration that cannot be individually attributed. This would seem to entail the introduction at the EC level of legislation with similarities to the US "Superfund" and with the objective of sharing responsibility for the costs of environmental restoration among the economic sectors most closely linked to the probable source of damage.

In March 1993 the Commission published for consultation its "Green Paper on Remedying Environmental Damage", which examines the usefulness of civil liability as a means for allocating responsibility for remedying environmental damage and for the costs of environmental restoration. The Green Paper also addresses the possibility of remedying environmental damage not covered by the application of civil liability principles by joint compensation schemes and raises the possibility that the EC might simply adopt the Council of Europe Convention on Liability for Environmental Damage.

Even though it is difficult to predict what legal form any future text on environmental liability will have, there is some indication that the Commission is considering a communication or recommendation on the subject, rather than a directive. This is due to the opposition of a majority within the Commission to a binding text.

Integrated Pollution Prevention and Control (IPPC)

In 1993 the Commission adopted a proposal for a directive on integrated pollution prevention and control. The principal aim of the proposed directive is to establish mechanisms in the member states to control the environmental impacts on air, water and soil when permits for certain industrial installations are issued. The proposal establishes minimum substantive requirements for appropriate emission standards but leaves it to the member states to determine individual emission values based on the state of technology. The proposal has been criticised in particular for providing the possibility of allowing higher emission values in individual

24

cases if the emission standards are generally met in a certain area. In 1995 the Council adopted a common position on a directive on IPPC, under which each permit has to prescribe emission standards for the installation in question which are based on the best available technology (BAT).

Indirect Approach

The Commission is eager to complement the existing "command-and-control" regulatory approach in the field of EC environmental law by indirect – *i.e.* financial and economic measures. These should incorporate into the prices of products the external costs or effects of the products and/or their production on the environment. Economic measures are expected to act as an incentive to improve compliance with environmental legislation and promote the use of best available technology.

However, the competence of the EC to introduce financial measures is limited. They can be based upon Arts. 130s, 100a, 99, 95 and 92 of the EC Treaty; the Maastricht Treaty introduced an explicit legal basis in Art. 130s.

According to the Fifth Action Programme, the Commission plans to introduce five types of economic measures:

- harmonisation of national charges and duties; there has been only a proposal for fees on road traffic;
- introduction of an "eco-tax"; the Commission has proposed an energy/eco-tax and taxation of bio-fuels, but new environmental taxes are seen as a threat to competitiveness of European industries; thus the Commission has called for an international approach; there have been plans for an eco-tax in the USA as well;
- standardisation of the current practice of member states in the field of environment subsidies with a focus on the polluter pays principle;
- development of accounting for environmental oriented factors in corporate accounts on the basis of eco-audits; and
- establishment of harmonised rules on liability.

International Environmental Law

The EC is increasingly participating in environmental measures and actions at the international level. The EC has signed the Basle Convention on the transborder movements of hazardous waste and intends to sign a protocol concerning emissions of volatile organic compounds and their transborder movements, attached to the Geneva Convention on Long-distance Transboundary Air Pollution.

The EC participated in the United Nations Conference on Environment and Development (UNCED) held in Rio de Janeiro in June 1992, at which a number of environmental conventions and programmes were adopted. The EC has on the whole expressed satisfaction with the results of the conference, and member states have in principle committed themselves to implement the measures agreed upon at the conference.

The EC intends to participate in a proposed framework convention on the protection and use of transborder waterways and international lakes. The EC has also become a member of the Baltic Commission, created to protect the environment and combat pollution of the Baltic Sea. Other members of the Baltic Commission are Estonia, Latvia, Lithuania, Denmark, Finland, Germany, Poland, Russia and Sweden.

The EC will also take an active part in the environmental programmes elaborated by the Council of Europe.

New Member States' Environmental Legislation

Austria, Finland and Sweden became member states in January 1995. Their environmental legislation is generally stricter than the legislation of the other member states, especially on standards of control of chemicals and pesticides. The new member states were allowed on accession to the EC to retain their stricter legislation until 1 January 1999. The Commission, however, has to produce proposals to revise the relevant directives by the end of this transition period, otherwise the stricter legislation will have to be harmonised down.

Chapter 2
Environmental Regulation in Belgium

Paul Herten
Baker & McKenzie, Brussels

Sources of Environmental Regulation

Constitutional Provisions

Belgium has now completed a process of constitutional reform which started more than 25 years ago with the first Constitutional Reform Act of 24 December 1970. In the course of this process the Belgian State has been reorganised as a federal union consisting of three autonomous regions: the Flemish and the Walloon Regions and the Region of Brussels (Art. 107 quater of the Belgian Constitution). A greater degree of legislative power and financial resources has been delegated to each of these regions. The Constitution itself provides only for the principle of delegation: the precise scope of the regional powers and their interaction with the residual federal powers are the subject of special statutes which require the approval of a majority within both the Dutch and the French speaking communities in parliament (Special Statute of 8 August 1980 as amended). It is generally believed that the constitutional reform will allow for better understanding and cooperation between the different regions within the federal framework of Belgium and of the European Community (EC). The legislative and fiscal powers of the three regions are likely to become even more important in the future.

Federal Statutes and Regional Decrees

As a result of this reform, all powers to regulate the environment have been transferred to the regional level. Only a few exceptional areas remain within the authority of the federal legislature: the formulation of product standards and product specifications (which, if not regulated on the federal level, could give rise to the creation of trade barriers between the regions), work, safety regulations and certain rules dealing with toxic and nuclear waste (Art. 6 of the Law of 8 August 1980).

This partitioning of powers has occasionally been criticised because it may lead to legal uncertainty and to an undue proliferation of regulations. A company doing business in Belgium needs to be familiar with environmental requirements which can be different in each of the three regions. These difficulties are in reality somewhat overstated since each region tends to follow initiatives and developments in the environmental field which the other regions introduce. The Flemish Region, for example, decided to abandon the licensing requirements which had existed on the national level merely as an aspect of the work safety regulations and to replace the "work safety" approach by a new comprehensive set of licensing rules, thereby introducing the concept of a single environmental permit (Decree of the Flemish Region of 28 June 1985 with the executive regulations known as VLAREM I and VLAREM II). This new attitude to environmental licensing was subsequently followed by a similar decree from the Brussels Region of 30 July 1992.

The risk of diverse or contradictory regulations is also reduced by the fact that the regional authorities in many environmental areas are required to comply with uniform international standards, specifically those imposed or recommended by the EC. Regional decrees will therefore refer to the same technical standards and requirements and ultimately have to implement on the regional level the same EC policies. For example, EC Directive 85/337 on the assessment of the impact which public or private projects may have on the environment has thus been implemented – separately but with substantially the same objectives – by the Walloon Region (Decrees of 11 September 1985 and 10 December 1987), by the Flemish Region (Decree of 23 March 1989) and by the Brussels

Region (Decree of 23 July 1992). International environmental law is becoming an increasingly important source for Belgian and regional legislators. Belgium also adheres to environmental initiatives taken within the framework of Benelux (conventions on the protection of animal species and landscaping), the Council of Europe, the OECD and the United Nations.

Administrative Procedures and Interpretations

Most environmental regulations are of relatively recent date and have therefore not yet become the subject of administrative guidelines or circulars. Such administrative interpretations or rulings would in any event not have a binding legal effect since only the courts have the power to interpret national or regional regulations.

Both federal and regional administrators are known to be responsive in dealing with environmental matters. Interested parties will often be able to obtain from the relevant officials informal advice or recommendations on the interpretation of the regulations and their application in a particular case. Even though such advice is not legally binding, it will for all practical purposes be considered as a reliable guideline for the interested parties.

It is worth noting in this connection that the Walloon Region (by Decree of 13 June 1991) and the Brussels Region (by Decree of 29 August 1991) have implemented EC Directive 90/313 providing for access to environmental information held by public authorities.

Relationship between National, Provincial and Local Regulations

The protection of the environment has in essence been delegated to the different regions. However, national rules or standards can be imposed or maintained in those areas where the regional authorities have not exercised their regulatory powers. The existence of national standards does not, however, prevent the regional authorities from imposing higher or stricter standards.

The provinces and municipalities play no role in formulating

29

environmental policies and regulations, although they have an important function in the administration of the licensing procedure.

Specific Laws and Regulations Applicable to Certain Areas of Environmental Regulation

Air Quality

The Law of 28 December 1964 as implemented by various decrees regulates the level of all emissions into the air capable of adversely affecting human health, plants, animals or property. The executive decrees provide as a minimum the emission standards imposed by EC directives. Higher standards have been introduced for more critical city areas or nature preservation areas. The decrees focus in particular on pollution by electric power stations and combustion plants. Only the Brussels Region has so far implemented the EC directive on the incineration of municipal and household waste (Decree of 31 May 1991).

Belgium has ratified and implemented the Geneva Convention on trans-border air pollution as well as the Vienna Convention (with the Montreal Protocol) for the protection of the ozone layer.

Water Quality

General water quality objectives have been set by a series of royal decrees issued under the Law of 24 May 1983. These general quality objectives have limited scope and relate only to drinking water, fishing areas and coastal zones. The objectives are in essence a transcript of the corresponding EC directives.

In addition, more stringent regulations exist for the protection of surface water and groundwater.

All public surface water is protected under the Law of 26 March 1971 as implemented by the Royal Decree of 3 August 1976. These national regulations have been supplemented in the different regions by decrees which generally impose higher standards and provide for more severe penalties (though also allowing in some instances for more flexible transition periods).

In general, the discharge of waste water into surface water, public sewers or artificial drains is prohibited unless a permit has been obtained from the relevant authority. An exception has been made for the discharge of domestic waste water into public sewers. The permit may refer to the special discharge conditions established for each industrial sector in order to take into account the specific needs or risks associated with each industry.

These sectoral conditions will be maintained for fixed periods of at least five years with a view to creating a level of security for the businesses involved.

As for groundwater, the Flemish Decrees of 24 January 1984 and 27 March 1985 require an operator to take all necessary measures to prevent pollution of the soil or of groundwater. This legislation (which seeks to implement EC Directive 80/68) also prohibits discharge of substances on the "black list" or "grey list" and requires a permit for over- or underground storage of such substances. Equivalent regulations have been adopted by the Walloon Region (Decrees of 30 April 1990 and 20 November 1991) and by the Brussels Region (Decrees of 18 September 1987 and 19 June 1989).

Waste

The Flemish Decree of 2 July 1981 as amended by Decree of 20 April 1994 regulates the management of all waste (except for nuclear or toxic waste). Every producer of waste is held responsible for its disposal either through the producer's own waste disposal unit or by transferring the waste to a licensed waste disposal operator. The waste producer or the disposal operator must give to the authorities on a quarterly basis detailed statistics and other information on the composition of the waste generated or collected and on its subsequent treatment or recycling. A special administrative body has been created (OVAM) to supervise the management of the entire process of waste generation, its disposal and treatment. The activities of OVAM are financed by special charges levied on all waste producers for amounts which are fixed for each category of waste.

In the Walloon Region, waste is regulated by the Decree of 5 July 1985, which focuses on the licensing aspects of the waste disposal process. The Walloon Region has not yet established a separate administrative body (such as OVAM) to deal in a comprehensive manner with the management of the entire waste process. On 30 October 1989 a five-year protocol was signed between the Flemish and the Walloon Regions for cooperation on waste disposal matters and for the prevention of unauthorised waste transfers from one region to the other. The Brussels Region has been late in developing its own regional initiative for waste management. However, by a Decree of 19 July 1990, Brussels created a Regional Agency for the promotion of a clean environment, and new initiatives in the area of waste reduction are expected.

As for toxic waste, the applicable legislation is still, by way of exception, national. The Law of 22 July 1974 and the Royal Decree of 9 February 1976 regulate the production and disposal of this type of waste. Any activity involving toxic waste (including production, sale, storage and export) must be reported to the competent authorities.

The 1974 Law also imposes a duty on a producer of toxic waste to destroy, neutralise or eliminate all such waste and provides for administrative and criminal sanctions as well as for strict civil liability if the producer fails to comply with this duty. Storage of toxic waste also requires a permit.

The importation, transit and export of waste, are regulated by an EC Regulation of 1 February 1993 which became directly applicable on 6 May 1994 and which in effect has replaced all earlier national and regional regulations on the subject.

Environmental Permitting Schemes

Permitting schemes are substantially different in each of the three Belgian regions.

In the Flemish Region, the regulations known as VLAREM I and VLAREM II have promoted the concept of a single, unitary environmental permit. The application for the permit covers all aspects of the activity concerned which may affect the environment (discharges into surface water, air emission standards, storage of waste, etc.). The Brussels Region has decided to adopt a similar approach. The Walloon Region still adheres to the procedures existing under the General Work Safety Regulations, which may require the applicant to file different permit applications with different authorities. The tendency in the Walloon Region is to improve the permitting process by creating new and updated licensing procedures for specific sectors of industry which are typical for the Walloon economy (such as mines, quarries, forest industry and tourism).

Notwithstanding this diversity, the regional permitting schemes have important features in common. The classified activities requiring a permit are divided into categories I and II. A permit for category I requires the approval of the provincial authorities, whilst a category II permit can be issued by the municipal authority. All regions require the relevant authority to decide on the application within narrowly defined time limits. The applicants or other interested parties have access to the administrative file and are entitled to an appeal procedure before the higher administrative authority. A final administrative appeal can be brought before the federal *Conseil d'Etat*. All regions provide for an advance and detailed evaluation of the project if the proposed activity might have a significant impact on the environment. The regional licensing authorities also require the applicant to demonstrate that his operations make use of the best available technology not entailing excessive costs. This principle is, however, not applied strictly for plants or activities which have already obtained their licence. Such existing operations will ordinarily be required to upgrade their technology only when their permit is renewed.

Enforcement of Environmental Regulations

Belgian environmental regulations provide for a legal framework which is generally considered to be adequate. EC directives and international initiatives are usually implemented in a timely fashion, and additional impetus has been given to the different regions as a result of the increased regulatory powers which they have received within the framework of recent constitutional reform.

The practical enforcement of environmental law is, however, very often criticised. Many regulations provide for administrative and criminal penalties which are not in proportion to the seriousness of the offence and are limited to a symbolic financial penalty. The regulations are also in some instances deficient and allow the operator to continue his polluting activity during the time-consuming administrative and judicial procedures.

A corporate entity can not be made the subject of criminal proceedings. Such proceedings can be brought only against the natural person who is responsible for the commission of the environmental offence. In any case, it can be difficult for the prosecution to demonstrate which person is actually responsible for the offence, so that a criminal prosecution may not succeed.

Important also is the problem of understaffing. Enforcement of environmental regulations is the responsibility of the administrative officials and of the public prosecutor's office in each district. The organisation of the regional administration is of recent date and many official positions are still vacant. Public prosecutors have so far shown limited interest in the prosecution of environmental violations. It is expected, however, that the administrative and judicial authorities will in the near future invest substantially more resources in more rigorous enforcement of environmental regulations.

Environmental Initiatives

Currently, much attention is paid to the issue of soil contamination. Inspired by precedent legislation in other EC jurisdictions (especially the Netherlands), the Flemish region promulgated a Decree on 23 February 1995 on the clean-up of contaminated soil (to come into force on 1 October 1996). The new regulation provides for the organisation of a public registry to identify all areas of contamination and, even more importantly, to prohibit the sale or transfer of any contaminated land unless the transferor has arranged for a prior clean-up of the contaminated site.

The issue of environmental management has also attracted much interest in the recent past, in the light of EC Regulation 1836/93 of 29 June 1993. Operators engaged in activities which may be critical from an environmental point of view will soon be required to develop manufacturing processes to better manage the impact of those activities on the environment. The performance of those companies in the environmental area will be monitored and evaluated by (voluntary) environmental audits, periodic emission reports and by internal environmental coordinators which those companies will have to appoint from within their own staff.

Chapter 3
Environmental Regulation in the Czech Republic

Marek J. Svoboda
Baker & McKenzie, Prague

Introduction

The former communist bloc countries in Central and Eastern Europe suffered a degree of environmental degradation unparalleled in modern times. The communist centrally planned economy exploited natural resources to the highest possible extent with little regard for the environment.

With the collapse of the Soviet system of government in Czechoslovakia in 1989, the legacy of environmental degradation became painfully obvious. A rediscovered environmental consciousness in government circles prompted the Civic Forum government of Vaclav Havel to embark upon an extensive programme of environmental legislation from 1990 to 1992. This was intended to establish a legal framework for the protection of the environment inspired by the principle of sustainable development instead of the unchecked exploitation of natural resources. The legislative programme has been extensive: between 1990 and 1995 14 new environmental acts were adopted by the parliament.

The split-up of Czechoslovakia on 1 January 1993 saw the creation of an independent Czech Republic. Following the demise of Civic Forum in the June 1992 elections and the extinction of the federal government in January 1993, the new coalition government led by the Civic Democratic Party of Vaclav Klaus has staunchly adhered (at least in public) to free market principles. The government has been much less keen on introducing new environmental regulations, anxious not to add to the economic burdens of Czech industry, nervous about survival in a competitive environment.

Sources of Environmental Regulation

Constitutional Provisions

According to the List of Fundamental Rights and Freedoms, which ranks on the level of the Czech Constitution, everyone has a right to live in an environment which is favourable to health and well-being. Citizens may assert this fundamental right before the courts against other private persons or public entities provided they have first exhausted all other legal remedies.

Acts, Decrees and Resolutions

The basic principles governing environmental protection are set out in the Act on the Environment No. 17/1992 Coll.

The preface to this act states that the legal framework for environmental protection is based on the fundamental principle of sustainable development: although man has the right to transform nature according to his design, he has the corresponding duty to do so in accordance with the principles of sustainable development, so that a favourable environment is preserved for future generations. The act imposes a general duty on every citizen to ensure that any part of the natural environment damaged by his or her action is restored to its original state.

There is also a general principle of law enshrined in the Civil Code that everyone has the duty to prevent damage to another's physical person and property, including any damage to the natural environment in which that person exists and from which he derives his wellbeing.

The other normative instruments which are used to regulate the environment include acts of Parliament (*Zakony*), ministerial decrees (*Vyhlásky*), government decrees (*Narìzeni vlády*), and resolutions (*Usnesení*). These instruments are used to regulate environmental problems in specific areas such as air pollution, exploitation of water resources, waste management and disposal and land development.

Environmental Authorities

There are three basic levels of environmental administration: the Ministry of Environment sets the broad principles of other government bodies. At the lower administrative level, districts, municipalities and local town councils (*Obce*) enforce minor environmental regulations and collect local charges on users of natural resources. The system is supplemented by environmental inspectorates. These are special state administrative bodies, existing at national (the Czech Environment Inspectorate) and regional level, which enforce the implementation of environmental norms and impose sanctions for infringement of these norms. The inspectorates may draw on the expertise of a number of expert bodies operating in the environmental area, such as the Czech Environmental Institute, the Czech Hydrometeorological Institute and the Water Research Institute.

In the first instance, the entity which has breached an environmental norm must account for its conduct to the responsible state authority. The level of the authority to which the entity is answerable depends on the seriousness of the breach. The environmental office of the district or local council investigates allegations involving minor offences. The most serious offences are investigated by the Ministry of Environment and the Czech Environment Inspectorate, which has authority to prosecute and to impose wide-ranging penalties.

In most cases, the responsibility for instituting proceedings for breach of environmental regulations is assigned by law to the inspectorates. The burden is on the defendant to prove that he did not cause or contribute to the environmental infringement. Proceedings instituted against a public authority are governed by the Administrative Code and not the Civil Code.

Specific Provisions Applicable to Certain Areas of Environmental Regulation

Air Quality

The legal protection of air quality is established by Act No. 309/1991 Coll. ("Clean Air Act") on protection of the air against pollutants, by Act No. 389/1991 Coll. on the responsibilities of the air protection authorities and the setting of emission charges (as amended by Act No. 212/1994), and by other implementing provisions. These acts contain emission limits for major air pollutants and lay down a time schedule within which industry is obliged to meet more stringent emission limits for listed pollutants. Existing pollution sources have to meet such standards by 1998. Ministerial Decree No. 41/1992 Coll. prescribes special air protection measures for certain areas most at risk from higher than average air pollution levels and sets the conditions to be met before a smog regulation system can be put into operation in any area at risk.

Measures 1 and 2 of the Air Emissions Act No. 84/1991 Coll. categorise activities according to source and industry and set emission limits based on the source and type of pollutant. Act No. 218/1992 defines the key terms of "new" and "existing" pollution sources and amended the Clean Air Act so as to oblige existing sources to meet the more stringent emission limits for new sources by 31 December 1998.

These normative measures are designed to encourage industry to invest in plant technology so as to lower emission levels below the limits set by regulation and at the least cost. However, the current charges imposed for failure to meet these limits or to do so within the time schedule set by the legislation are too low to induce reduction of emissions or investment in clean air technology. The government anticipates, however, that up to 75% of all plants will be able to meet the new stringent limits by the end of 1998. Limits for emissions from mobile sources are laid down in Act No. 41/1984 Coll. (as amended by Act No. 248/1991 Coll.).

No. 86/1991 Coll. on the Protection of the Ozone Layer has introduced provisions for the Czech Republic to comply with international commitments to reduce the use of ozone-depleting substances set by the Montreal Protocol 1987. To meet these commitments the import of fluorocarbons has been banned with effect from the beginning of 1996.

Water Quality

The provisions for the protection of surface water and groundwater and for the management of water resources are contained in the basic Act on Water No. 138/1973 Coll. and subsequent provisions. This act generally regulates the use and management of water resources and sets water quality standards. The water management authorities administer compliance with the duties set out in the act on maintenance of water resources. The regulatory system is based on a charging system for failure to comply with such duties, *e.g.* excessive extraction of water or discharge of waste into public waters. The level of the charge is, however, not sufficient to promote more sparing extraction of water. More fundamentally, the act does not clearly define property rights in water, so that it remains difficult to assign obligations for damage to the water environment.

In addition, the Water Act No. 171/1992 Coll. attempts to define the legally permissible content of polluting substances in water. It leaves many areas unregulated, however, particularly the discharge of chemical substances.

Waste Management

The legal norms are contained in the Act on Waste Management No. 238/1991 Coll. The act outlines the substantive rights and obligations of those producing and handling waste and procedures for its management. The act recognises two broad categories of waste: hazardous (special) waste and ordinary waste. It also sets out the responsibilities of the state administrative authorities for waste management. The importation of waste for disposal in the Czech Republic is prohibited unless it complies with a regime of conditions. Every entity producing waste is obliged to formulate a waste management programme, and there is a substantial penalty for non-compliance.

Waste regulation is based on a charging system but, as with the other environmental media, the charges are too low to serve as incentives for beneficial change in the economic conduct of industrial waste producers; they often have the opposite effect in encouraging the illicit tipping of waste. There are also no incentives for the collection, salvage or recycling of waste.

In December 1995, an amendment to the Act on Waste Management No. 238/1991 Coll. and to the Act on State Administration of Waste No. 311/1991 Coll., as amended, was adopted, defining those properties of waste which would put it in the category of hazardous waste. An authorised inspector accredited by the Ministries of Environment and Health must assess whether the waste in question has any of the specified properties. The list of hazardous properties appears as an annexe to the amended Act on Waste Management.

Development of Land and Environmental Impact Assessment

Act No. 244/1992 Coll. on Environmental Impact Assessment obliges the proposer of any construction project, land development or production, exploitation or importation of technology of any size or significance to prepare a report on its wider impact upon the local environment. Many of the provisions of this act mirror the EC Environmental Impact Assessment Directive. The act does not, however, cover products and their life-cycles, planning concepts or the transboundary impacts of projects.

A new Forestry Act No. 289/1995 Coll. was also adopted at the end of 1995.

Environmental Initiatives during the Privatisation Process

During the privatisation process of large industry every project was required to undergo an environmental audit. The proposer of the privatisation project had to file a report on the environmental liabilities of the industrial enterprise with a special governmental committee before the privatisation project could be approved.

An indemnity fund was also set up by Parliament in 1993 to finance the cost of environmental clean up of sites belonging to privatised enterprises. The fund is available to indemnify companies for the actual cost of the clean-up measures proposed in an environmental audit. The cost must not exceed the purchase price of the privatised enterprise, and the environmental audit must be performed by an environmental consultancy approved by the Ministry of Environment.

Enforcement of Environmental Regulations

Civil Liability for Environmental Damage

The Act on the Environment imposes a general duty on every citizen to remedy any environmental damage caused by persons or legal entities. If remedy is not possible the duty is to compensate society in some other way. As a general principle of law, compensatory damages may be awarded against any person or legal entity who does not remedy environmental damage caused by them.

There is a general obligation in the Civil Code on every citizen to act in such a way as to avoid damaging human health, property and the natural environment. An entity may therefore be held strictly liable for breaching an environmental norm which causes damage, and a plaintiff does not have to prove fault. Civil damages may only be awarded to those who can prove that they suffered environmental damage caused by the conduct complained of. There is also a corresponding obligation on the injured party to mitigate his losses wherever possible. Injunctive relief is also available in the courts against the imminent danger or threat of damage to the environment.

Strict Liability for Damage under the Civil Code

In the course of operating a business and in other circumstances such as the transport or handling of hazardous substances a defendant will be strictly liable for any damage which he caused to another's person or property. He can avoid liability only if he can prove that the damage was caused by an unavoidable event not connected with his activity. Carriers of dangerous substances may similarly only escape liability for damage resulting from an accident during transport if they can prove that they made every possible effort to avoid the accident.

Joint and Several Liability

Under the Civil Code where several entities are found to have contributed to environmental damage, any one of them may be held liable for the entirety of the damage. Only a court of law may apportion liability for such damage as between the defendants on their relative degrees of fault.

In commercial transactions and in some types of commercial contract the Commercial Code will apply to the contract between the parties, with the provisions of the Civil Code playing a supplementary role. In such cases, the parties may determine the extent of their environmental and other liabilities differently than as provided in the Code. The general principle remains, however, that the defendant is liable for compensatory damages for any act or omission which caused damage to the person or property of the other party. No party can agree to waive its rights to damages resulting from breach of any right which may accrue to him in the future. The level of damages may, however, be negotiated in the contract terms.

Statute of Limitations

The general limitation on bringing civil actions is three years from the date on which the claims could first have been asserted. The right to claim compensation for damage resulting from an unintentional act becomes statute-barred two years after the injured party first became aware of the damage. In the case of damage to property resulting from an intentional act, the claim becomes statute-barred ten years after the occurrence of the damage. The court is not obliged to address the statute of limitations issue if it is not raised by the defendant.

Criminal Sanctions

Infringement of an environmental regulation constitutes an environmental misdemeanour for which the defendant will be strictly liable and will have a fine imposed. Criminal liability may also result under the Criminal Code No. 140/1961 Coll. when serious harm is done to the environment intentionally or as a result of criminal negligence or there is a serious threat of harm from an intentional or grossly negligent act. Criminal sanctions can also be imposed upon businesses for breach of environmental regulations. Fines may be imposed for intentional, reckless or criminally negligent conduct which results in permanent harm to the environment as well as for failing to mitigate damage, or failure to report to the state inspectorate environmental damage or any threat of such damage. There are maximum levels of fine which may be imposed by the environmental inspectorate under the Act on the Environment.

Government Environmental Policy

The environmental policy of the government is outlined annually in a report presented to Parliament. In the October 1995 report the government stated that although air and water pollution levels had been significantly reduced mainly because of lower industrial production, its current goals would be to transfer more environmental costs from the state to the private sector and to raise environmental standards by the year 2005 to those which existed in the EC in 1990.

In line with government policy of reducing state subsidies for environmental compliance and ensuring that the private sector assumes the full cost of meeting its environmental obligations, the resources from environmental charges are being channelled away from the state budget into a special environmental fund. The purpose of the fund is to provide soft loans and limited grants for private sector projects which would not otherwise be commercially viable. However, as industry begins to meet more stringent environmental standards fewer charges will be collected and the fund will diminish. The government therefore expects that the role of the fund will shift to the provision of financial guarantees and reduced interest loans in order to mobilise financial resources for purposes of environmental protection. As this trend continues, the main cost of environmental compliance will be borne by the polluter, following the polluter pays principle. This is likely to continue as the official environmental policy for the foreseeable future.

Chapter 4
Environmental Regulation in Egypt

Samir M. Hamza
Baker & McKenzie, Cairo

Sources of Environmental Regulation

Constitutional Provisions

The present constitution of the Arab Republic of Egypt is that of 11 September 1971, as amended on 22 May 1980. The Constitution makes no direct reference to the government's authority to regulate the environment, although such authority is accepted as implicit to the proper management of the state.

Statutes, Public Laws, Presidential Decrees, International Treaties

Egyptian environmental legislation is primarily the product of laws approved by the People's Assembly (the Egyptian equivalent of parliament). The President of the Republic may also issue decrees in cases of necessity or exceptional circumstances, and these have the force of law upon authorisation from the People's Assembly.

Egypt is party to several international treaties concerning environmental protection. Under the Constitution, treaties once ratified by the People's Assembly are part of Egypt's internal legislation.

Civil law can also be used to protect the environment. The Civil Code (Article 163) stipulates that liability arising from wrongful acts (torts) creates an obligation on the tortfeasor to make reparation to the injured party. Injunctions may be issued in exceptional cases where irreparable harm is being caused to the environment.

Executive Regulations or Administrative Interpretations

Executive regulations are issued by the relevant ministers in accordance with laws passed by the People's Assembly and presidential decrees. Executive regulations take the form of guidelines prepared for the purpose of implementing such laws or decrees.

The administrative interpretation of laws and executive regulations is also the responsibility of the relevant minister. Ministers may publish additional guidelines or codes of practice that are of assistance in understanding the applications of any given law or decree.

Administrative interpretations may be challenged either by a procedure detailed in the relevant law and the executive regulations or in certain instances in the courts.

National Regulation

Laws enacted by the People's Assembly and presidential decrees have force throughout Egypt. The monitoring and enforcement of environmental legislation is carried out on a national level with little responsibility left to regional authorities. Enforcement is carried out by the appropriate ministry responsible for applying the law dealing with the specific matter in question.

Specific Provisions, Laws, Executive Regulations and Presidential Decrees Applicable to Certain Areas of Environmental Regulation

A new and comprehensive era in Egyptian environmental regulation commenced on 3 February 1994 with the introduction of

Law No. 4 of 1994 ("the Law"). The Law encompasses almost all previous environmental legislation covering land, air and water, providing administrative and judicial procedures, penalties for violations and establishing a single executive agency, the Agency for Environmental Affairs (AEA) charged with implementation of the Law. An important surviving previous law, however, is Law No. 48 of 1982 for the protection of the River Nile.

The Law allows three years for existing entities to achieve compliance, with a possible further two years at the discretion of the appropriate governmental bodies.

The Law also provides for a system of incentives to persons or entities who carry out works or projects to protect the environment. The system is to be established by the AEA, approved by its board of directors and ratified by the Prime Minister.

Air Quality

The Law provides in general terms for limits and controls on the emission of pollutants into the air as well as for noise. The limits are by reference to designated areas as well as to single sources. Specific levels of pollutants are set out in executive regulations under the Law.

Emissions above limits prescribed in executive regulations from machines, engines or vehicles are prohibited. Offenders may be subject to a fine, and the operators' licence may be suspended and, in the event of recurring violation, cancelled.

The emission of particles into the air during exploration, mining, landscaping or demolition and the transport of waste or earth from such operations are controlled. Furthermore, entities involved in such operations must take all necessary precaution for the safe storage and transport of such wastes or earth. Offenders may be subject to a fine and suspension of the operator's licence.

Entities engaged in the exploration and drilling for and development, extraction, production, refining and processing of crude oil must comply with international industry standards as determined by the appropriate government bodies.

The Law makes detailed provisions about the conditions of health in the work environment: control of emissions, overall exposure of employees, the provision of protective gear, setting permissible temperature and humidity levels and ventilation requirements.

Smoking is prohibited in all enclosed public places unless specifically allowed under licence and then only in accordance with the relevant executive regulations under the Law and in designated smoking areas.

The Law also regulates the overall radioactive level and/or the concentration of radioactive substances in the environment.

Protection of the Marine Environment

The provisions of the Law protecting the marine environment are divided into protection from pollution from ships and from land-based pollution. The method of control is by imposition of a penalty and in particular cases by payment of damages and by requirement to clean up. Entities involved in the exploration for exploitation and drilling of off-shore oilfields and other natural resources, captains of ships and entities engaged in operations which result in land-based marine pollution can be held jointly liable for all fines, third party damages and clean up costs resulting from violations of the Law.

There are comprehensive provisions prohibiting dumping of potentially harmful materials into territorial waters. In addition, there are detailed provisions prohibiting oil-based marine pollution. The dumping of oil or oil mixtures is prohibited. Offenders may be subject to a fine and financial responsibility for all necessary clean-up. Businesses involved in the exploration, drilling and exploitation of and extraction from off-shore oilfields and operation of platforms and the retrieval of other natural resources from territorial waters are prohibited from discharging waste into the sea and must treat such waste by the latest methods complying with international standards. Offenders may be subject to a fine. The authorities have power to require owners or captains of ships to take safety precautions to prevent an environmental crisis. The Law strictly forbids the discharge or disposal of sanitary waste and garbage from ships and off-shore platforms. Such waste must be disposed of in accordance with procedures indicated in executive regulations under the Law, although the actual method and place of disposal is left to the discretion of the relevant administrative authority.

As for operations which may result in land-based pollution of the sea, there are licensing requirements and powers to the authorities to investigate and to implement necessary measures in a crisis, with fines for offenders. The licence will be granted only following an environmental impact study and implementation of any measures necessary to prevent pollution. All installations, whether public, commercial, industrial, tourist or service establishments, are prohibited from discharging or disposing of any materials, waste or untreated liquids which are liable to pollute the shore or the adjacent sea. Offenders may be subject to a fine for each day the non-compliance continues. The Law also contains zoning requirements for construction on the shore, to be enforced by independent local inspectors. In case of non-compliance, the entity concerned is required to come into compliance or may be subject to a restraining order which will require the site to be restored to its original state.

The River Nile and the Fresh Water Environment

Law No. 48 of 1982 for the protection of the River Nile and its waterways from pollution regulates the discharge of wastes into these waters and the use of agrochemicals or herbicides used to fight water weeds in order to safeguard these waters for irrigation purposes. Moreover, this Law covers not only the River Nile but all fresh water in Egypt. The Law defines fresh water as the River Nile, its two branches, fresh water canals, drains, lakes and aqueducts. The Law also prohibits the discharge of waste into these waters, except pursuant to a permit from the Ministry of Public Works and Irrigation. This permit is granted only after certain criteria have been met by the applicant, who is monitored on a regular basis to ensure compliance with the set criteria. The Law also requires houseboats, tourist boats and cargo ships to arrange for the treatment of their wastes and forbids the release of these wastes into the River Nile. Finally, the Law prohibits the mixture of agricultural drainage water with fresh water unless certain criteria are met.

Waste and Hazardous Materials

Hazardous waste is defined by executive regulations and the Law in substantially the same terms as those of the Basle Convention, which Egypt has signed. The regulations also require the relevant ministers to issue a table of hazardous waste and materials.

The Law requires all entities engaged in the production, use, disposal or handling of waste and hazardous materials to be licensed. The licence is granted by the relevant administrative authority after consulting the AEA. The location of sites for the disposal of hazardous waste is determined by the Ministry of Housing after consulting the Ministries of Health and Industry as well as the AEA. The location of sites for the disposal of solid waste by incineration, dumping or treatment is determined by the relevant local government units, subject to the advice and consent of the AEA.

Entities involved in the production, circulation or handling of hazardous materials, whether in their solid, liquid or gaseous state, must take all precautions to prevent any damage from such materials to the environment. They must maintain a register of such wastes, the method of disposal, records of the facilities and authorities under contract for disposal and transport of such wastes.

The Law prohibits importation of hazardous waste, including entry of such waste for the purpose of transit. However, ships may enter territorial waters while carrying hazardous waste provided they have the appropriate licence from the relevant administrative authority.

Offenders may be punished by a fine or imprisonment, and offenders under the prohibition on importation may be required to re-export at their own expense the hazardous waste wrongfully imported.

Protection of Land

An application for a construction licence requires a statement of environmental impact. The application and the statement are evaluated by the authority considering the application but subject to the ultimate approval of the AEA. There is a right of appeal under the implementing executive regulations.

The owner and operator of an establishment is under an affirmative duty to monitor the environmental impact of the establishment. In addition, the network of survey teams of the AEA carry out inspections for compliance, and the AEA monitors the records kept by the establishment. The procedures are set out in executive regulations. Enforcement is by the AEA. Offenders will have a 60-day period for compliance, and in default the consequences can include the imposition of penalties, an administrative injunction to cease the offending activity and a charge for the expenses of restoring the area damaged.

The AEA is to design contingency plans for natural disasters, including establishment of a command and control centre in the event of such a disaster and to head a task force with all necessary powers. It is also to collect information so as to evaluate areas of potential environmental crisis.

The Agency for Environmental Affairs

The creation of the AEA is intended to cure the previous ineffective operation of previous laws because of a chaotic structure for implementation and enforcement. The AEA is managed by a board of directors, chaired by the Minister for the Environment. It is an independent body with its own budget and the power to establish branches throughout the country.

Administrative and Judicial Procedures under the Law

The Law sets out administrative and judicial procedures to be followed under it. The Minister of Justice and other relevant ministries have power to appoint investigating officers. Representatives of other relevant administrative authorities and consular representatives abroad are deemed to be investigating officers. Such officers can conduct independent on-site inspections to ensure compliance and can require investigated entities to provide all available relevant information. The relevant administrative authority issues its decisions on the basis of these investigations and will set out the steps necessary to protect the environment. An appeal is possible to the Complaints Committee, although an appeal may not stay enforcement.

Penalties and Procedures for Enforcement of the Law

The Law makes detailed provisions for the various penalties for offences and the procedures for imposing them. The penalties are essentially fines, with the possible imposition of criminal sanctions as well. The maximum penalty is imprisonment with hard labour for 25 years for the most serious offences (*i.e.* those involving the death of three or more persons). The Law also defines the parties potentially liable and the extent of their liability. The Law also provides that imposition of a penalty under the Law shall not preclude the imposition of any stricter penalty prescribed in other legislation.

Whilst the Law does not contain a "whistle-blowing" provision, it does reserve rights of enforcement to individuals and to non-governmental organisations, thus including organisations within Egypt's developing "Green Movement".

Chapter 5
Environmental Regulation in England and Wales

Thomas Handler*
Baker & McKenzie, London

Sources of Environmental Regulation

Constitutional Provisions

This outline covers England and Wales only, not any other part of the United Kingdom.

The United Kingdom and its parts have no written constitution.

It is accepted that European Community (EC) law, including regulations, directives, whether implemented or by the doctrine of direct effect, and judgments of the European Court of Justice are part of English law.

Statutes, Public Laws

Environmental regulation is increasingly by statutes, which in turn increasingly have origins in EC law. Parliament passes statutes (*e.g.* the Environmental Protection Act 1990 (EPA 1990) and the Environment Act 1995 (EA 1995)). Statutes, *e.g.* the EPA 1990 and the EA 1995, can be in broad framework terms, with detail fleshed out in regulations under the statutes, guidance notes, etc., and are brought into force in stages. The government can indicate its legislative intent in a White Paper (*e.g.* the White Paper on the Environment of September 1990 on which the government has

*The author gratefully acknowledges the assistance of Susan Pluckrose (Baker & McKenzie, London) in the preparation of this chapter.

reported annually). The Department of the Environment (DoE) has the major role in formulating the government's policies. The activities of the government are scrutinised by Parliamentary Select Committees.

The criminal law is important in environmental regulation and is largely created by statutes.

The common law torts developed by the civil courts over the years are also important. These include nuisance (broadly, unreasonable interference with the use of land), negligence (broadly, failure to take reasonable care causing foreseeable damage), *Rylands* v *Fletcher* liability (strict liability for the escape of dangerous things brought onto land) and trespass (broadly, interference with or encroachment on rights). These torts give persons and entities rights to claim damages and injunctions for damage or injury suffered by them.

Regulations or Administrative Interpretations

Regulations are made by the relevant ministers under powers granted by statutes and approved by Parliament. Guidelines, guidance notes and codes of practice may be provided for under statute and are important. They are published by the government, often following consultation with interested parties and the public. The government also publishes circulars and policy documents which are also important. Administrative interpretations of statutes and regulations are by the relevant authorities.

Administrative interpretations may be challenged either by the procedure that may be laid down in the statute or in the court by judicial review (for exceeding powers, unreasonable exercise of discretion or procedural unfairness). Maladministration not challengeable in any other way may give rise to a complaint to the ombudsman.

Relationship between National, Provincial and Local Regulation

The laws of the United Kingdom differ as between (1) England and Wales, (2) Scotland, and (3) Northern Ireland; broadly speaking, environmental regulation is similar in all parts, the difference being the greatest between Scotland and the rest. England and Wales are effectively one state and there are no provinces. Regulation is, broadly speaking, uniform for England and Wales, although there is significant decentralisation and for example, the Environment Agency ("the Agency") operates in a number of regions. Local authorities regulate their own areas in accordance with statutes – including in important matters such as air quality, noise and aspects of contaminated land, as well as planning and public health. Some standards may be set locally and are therefore variable (*e.g.* for emissions permissible in the light of local conditions), others are set nationally.

Specific Provisions, Statutes and Regulations Applicable to Certain Areas of Environmental Regulation

Air Quality

The regime governing air quality is most importantly contained in the EPA 1990 and the EA 1995, with significant regulations, guidance notes and other guidance issued by the government (*e.g.* Integrated Pollution Control – A Practical Guide).

The EPA 1990 controls air quality in two ways: by integrated control and by local authority control.

The regime of Integrated Pollution Control (IPC) is a cross-media system of control of discharges to land and water as well as to air and requires authorisation to operate prescribed more heavily polluting processes ("Part A" processes, covering the fuel and power, chemical, minerals, metal, waste disposal and certain other industries). Regulations define the processes and substances, establish emission standards, limit values, quality objectives and allocation of quotas. Authorisation is by the Agency, which is also the enforcing authority. Authorisation may be subject to conditions, and every authorisation is subject to the requirement to use the best available techniques not entailing excessive cost (BATNEEC) to prevent or minimise releases of prescribed substances. If substances are released into more than one environmental medium, the process must take the best practicable environmental option available.

Processes (specified "Part B" processes) and substances with a lower pollution potential are subject – but only for their impact on air – to separate though similar control by authorisation from the local authorities.

The EA 1995 from 1 April 1997 brings into operation a framework air quality management system. There will be a national strategy for air quality implemented in two ways. The first is by air quality standards for nine pollutants (ozone, sulphur dioxide, particulates, etc.) with guideline and more serious alert thresholds, as well as timetables for achieving objectives. The second is by local air quality management areas administered by local authorities, who will be under a duty to carry out assessments and to take action in identified areas to achieve required objectives.

Local authorities are also under a duty to enforce the Clean Air Act 1993 which prohibits emissions of dark smoke, grit and dust from chimneys of buildings and chimneys of furnaces of fixed boilers or industrial plant. Under the act local authorities are also responsible for ensuring that furnaces and chimneys meet specified design criteria and an authority may declare all or part of its area to be a "smoke control area".

The Health and Safety at Work etc. Act 1974 imposes a general duty on persons in control of prescribed premises to use the best practicable means to prevent emission of noxious or offensive substances or to render them harmless. This duty is general and not limited to protecting the health and safety of those present at the premises. The duty is enforced by the Health and Safety Executive. Regulations under the act are significant.

Emissions to air can also be statutory nuisances, regulated by the EPA 1990. A statutory nuisance must be something prejudicial to health or a nuisance at common law and may relate to smoke, fumes, gases or noise from premises or dust, steam, smell or other effluvia from industrial or business premises. Local authorities must inspect their districts and serve an abatement notice on the person responsible, who must comply unless he can show that he had used the best practicable means to try to avoid the nuisance.

It may be noted here that the basic control over noise is also the statutory nuisance regime.

Water Quality

Water quality is regulated essentially by control of emissions into water and by setting of water quality objectives.

The Water Act 1989 regulated the provision of water supplies and the disposal of effluent, as well as establishing the new structure of the water industry: water companies (privatised) to supply water (including wholesome water for drinking purposes) and to deal with sewage (including making improvements and providing for the disposal of trade effluent); and an independent National Rivers Authority to control water pollution and to grant consents to discharge into controlled waters (effectively all water, including groundwater).

The Water Act 1989 has been superseded by five acts which consolidate most of the relevant water legislation; the most important of the new acts are the Water Resources Act 1991 (WRA 1991) and the Water Industries Act 1991 (WIA 1991). The National Rivers Authority has been superseded by the Agency.

The control of emissions into water is by prohibition of pollution and a system of consents.

The prohibition is by the general pollution offence under the WRA 1991 of causing or knowingly permitting polluting matter or solid waste to enter water. The defences include a statutory discharge consent and an IPC authorisation. Conversely, discharge to water contrary to an IPC authorisation is prohibited under the EPA 1990 (*e.g.* of "Red List" substances, dangerous substances listed in the Trade Effluents (Prescribed Processes and Substances) Regulations 1989 amended by the 1990 Regulations). Other pollution offences include the offence under the Salmon and Freshwater Fisheries Act 1975 of causing or knowingly permitting any matters to be put into water so as to cause it to be poisonous to fish. Water pollution may involve a statutory nuisance under the EPA 1990 or under the Public Health Act 1936.

Complementing the pollution offences are important provisions under the WRA 1991 to prevent pollution. The Agency has widely drawn powers to prevent pollution where this is threatened, to carry out works to this end and to recover the cost from the person who caused or knowingly permitted the pollution or the threat of pollution. These powers are being supplemented by the works notice procedure introduced into the WRA 1991 by the EA 1995 (see below under Waste Generation, contaminated land). The WRA 1991 also contains powers for designating water protection zones and nitrate sensitive areas and for regulations for precautions against pollution, and regulations have been made to cover silage, slurry and agricultural fuel oil.

The system of consents to discharge is operated by the Agency. Application is made for each discharge, generally this is publicised and a fee is to be paid. The consent is granted to a named person or entity and it may be subject to conditions which may take into account water quality objectives, EC standards, etc. Consents may be revoked or varied and enforcement notices can be served for breaches of consent. Appeals are possible. There is a public register of applications, consents, discharge samples, etc., but information prejudicing a trade secret or the public interest may be excluded. Broadly similar to the control of emissions to water is the control of trade effluent discharges under the WIA 1991. In addition to the Trade Effluents (Prescribed Processes and Substances) Regulations 1989 and 1990 the 1992 Regulations create special category effluents. Discharges of trade effluent from trade premises (both broadly defined) are prohibited unless a trade effluent consent is given by a sewerage undertaker. The consent is normally granted subject to conditions and payment of effluent charges. There is a public register as for water but discharge samples are not shown.

The IPC regime under the EPA 1990 takes water quality into account, particularly the release of prescribed substances from prescribed processes – the "Red List" substances.

The setting of water quality objectives was first formulated in 1989 and is now contained in the WRA 1991. The process is at an early stage and is expected to take some years to accomplish. The process involves:

- regulations establishing standards for water to bring it within classification; regulations have been made for surface water (including drinking water), bathing water, river ecosystems and dangerous substances;
- setting water quality objectives incorporating the relevant standard for individual stretches of water; considerable public consultation is involved at this stage; and

- the Agency having a duty to achieve and maintain the water quality so far as practicable; this will be reflected in the Agency's attitude to granting discharge consents.

Waste Generation

The basic policies of managing the generation of waste (to tackle it at source, to prevent and minimise it and to dispose of it safely) are included in a formal National Waste Strategy established by the EA 1995. When in force, the strategy is expected to replace local plans and meet EC requirements for waste management plans. The policies are backed by regulations and economic instruments, in particular recycling credits and the landfill tax.

Waste disposal on land has always required planning permission, but the most significant legislation is the EPA 1990 for waste management and the EA 1995 for packaging waste and contaminated land.

Waste is defined as controlled or Directive waste in the EPA 1990 and in 1994 regulations in accordance with the EC Waste Directive 1991. The EPA 1990 also separated the operational (*e.g.* waste collection) and the regulatory roles of the local waste authorities (the latter role now assumed by the Agency).

The basic prohibition is on the improper disposal of waste. This prohibition is supplemented by an important "cradle to grave" duty of care on anyone who imports, produces, carries, keeps, treats or disposes of waste. The duty is to take all reasonable measures to prevent the unauthorised handling of waste or its escape from control and to secure that any transfer of such waste is only to an authorised person. All waste carriers must be licensed. Unusually for a duty to take reasonable measures, breach is a criminal offence. A government code of practice sets out matters to assist compliance.

The basic control under the new system is on those who produce or deal with waste, and these activities require a waste management licence for deposit, treatment, keeping or disposal of waste. Manufacturers who keep quantities of waste from their production pending disposal elsewhere do not need a licence, provided that the quantities are small and that special (*i.e.* particularly dangerous or intractable) waste is securely kept until disposal.

The system of waste management licensing is operated by the Agency. Licences may be granted subject to conditions, which in the case of site licences continue to apply after closure of the site. Local authority planning permission must be in force and the Health and Safety Executive must consent. The applicant for the licence must be fit and proper to hold the licence and the operation must not cause pollution or harm to health. The Agency retains full control over the licence and is under a duty to supervise. It may modify, suspend or revoke a licence, and a site licence may be surrendered only if the Agency accepts it, which the Agency can do only after inspection of the site to see if it may cause pollution or harm to health. Fees are payable on the application for the licence and annually, and there is a public register of a wide range of information on the waste management licensing regime.

The Agency has power to require the owner or occupier of land to remove waste deposited in breach of a prohibition. Failure to comply is an offence and entitles the Agency to carry out the removal and recover its costs. The rights of appeal under the regime are to the Secretary of State. The EPA 1990 also imposes civil liability for damage caused by unlawful deposit of waste.

Special waste (defined as waste "so dangerous or difficult to dispose of" as to require special provisions) is subject to the basic regime applying to all waste, but is also controlled by the Control of Pollution (Special Waste) Regulations 1980 made under the Control of Pollution Act 1974. The producer of special waste must create a series of consignment notes to be passed to the carriers and the disposers, with copies to the Agency. The disposers must keep site records, including a record of the location of each deposit. On 1 September 1996 new Special Waste Regulations 1996 came into force, implementing the EC Hazardous Waste Directive 1991. The new regulations broaden the definition of special waste and determine whether consignment notes are required to notify the Agency in advance of movements of special waste and require fuller description of such waste and its hazards.

The EPA 1990 also gives the Secretary of State power, so as to prevent pollution or harm to human health, to prohibit or restrict the import or export of waste and the import and use of any specified substance.

The EC Packaging and Packaging Waste Directive 1994 will be implemented by a shared approach to producer responsibility, supported by regulations under the EA 1995. The aim is that the targets under the directive (recovery of 50–65% and recycling of 25–45% of packaging waste by 2001) be met by apportioning the obligations for waste minimisation to the organisations in all four sectors in the packaging chain. The regulations are expected to impose obligations to be met by the organisations themselves or through joining a scheme. The recovery and recycling target is likely to be 58%, and there are likely to be exemptions for businesses using less than 50 tonnes of packaging in the year (which should exempt some 90% of all businesses).

Clean-up of contaminated land may be achieved directly or indirectly in a variety of ways: as a statutory nuisance under the EPA 1990, as adversely affecting amenity under the Town and Country Planning Act 1990, as pollution of water under the WRA 1991, as unlawful deposit of waste under the EPA 1990, and under the common law torts of negligence, nuisance or *Rylands* v *Fletcher*. In practice clean-up has also been achieved on development or redevelopment of land as a condition of planning consent.

The EA 1995 makes important new provisions for clean-up of contaminated land (inserting these into the EPA 1990) and of polluted water (inserting these into the WRA 1991). These provisions are likely to come into force in 1997 and late in 1996 respectively.

Local authorities are under a duty to inspect their areas in order to identify "contaminated land". Once they identify such land, they and the Agency have to consider whether it ought to be designated as a "special site". The authorities must serve an identification notice on every owner and occupier of the land and on every "appropriate person", informing them that the land is contaminated. Unless there is an imminent danger of serious harm or serious water pollution, a three month consultation period follows service of the notice. During this period the authorities and notified persons have to determine what remediation must be carried out. At the expiration of the period, the authorities must serve a "remediation notice" on each appropriate person, specifying what has to be done by way of remediation and within what time period. Failure to comply with a remediation notice is a criminal offence. The authorities may carry out the work at their own cost and recover this from the appropriate persons, taking account of any serious hardship this might cause. There is a right of appeal.

The authorities are under a duty to keep public registers, which will record, for example, remediation notices, notification of completed remediation and convictions.

The statutory provisions will be supplemented by guidance and regulations to detail the manner in which the authorities should go about inspecting their areas; to define what would constitute contaminated land; to define what would constitute significant harm and a special site; to detail the mode of identification of appropriate persons and allocation and apportionment of responsibilities between appropriate persons if more than one.

Definitions are important:

"Contaminated land" is land in such a condition by reason of substances in, on or under it, that significant harm is being or is likely to be caused, or that pollution of water is being or is likely to be caused.

"Special site" is not defined in the statute but is expected to cover land which, by reason of substances in, on or under it, would or might cause serious harm or serious pollution of water.

"Harm" means harm to the health of living organisms, interference with ecological systems and harm to owned property.

"Remediation" includes assessment of harm; prevention, minimisation, clean-up and restoration of a site, adjacent land and water; and monitoring after clean-up. Only proportional and reasonable remedial action, based on a cost-benefit analysis, can be required.

"Appropriate persons" are a hierarchy: any person who caused or knowingly permitted the contamination, but if after reasonable inquiry no such person has been found, the owner or occupier of the land for the time being.

In a separate "works notice" procedure the Agency may require the person who caused or knowingly permitted water pollution to take remedial action at his own cost. This represents a substantial addition to existing powers under the WRA 1991, whereby the

Agency has to carry out the work at its own cost and can only then seek to recover those costs. The works notice procedure offers fewer safeguards to polluters than the remediation notice procedure and is easier to exercise. The relationship between the two procedures may be clarified by guidance and by practice.

Environmental Permitting Schemes

Procedures

The general scheme is for application to the relevant authority, made in writing and accompanied by the required fee. The decision of the authority is generally subject to review under the statute. The procedures vary in detail, although some element of publicity is generally involved. The following outline is given of the IPC regime under the EPA 1990 as an example.

Application is made to the Agency on the prescribed form. Details must be given of the applicant, the plant, the prescribed process and substances, the techniques to prevent or reduce the release of prescribed or other harmful substances, proposals for monitoring releases and evidence that the applicant will use BATNEEC.

Fees are set annually. The current fee to accompany the application is calculated by multiplying a flat-rate fee of £3,860 by the number of components in the process, and the current annual subsistence charge is calculated by multiplying a flat rate fee of £1,805 by the number of components.

The applicant must advertise the application in a local newspaper and the London Gazette giving specified details and inviting the public to inspect the application and make any representations to the Agency.

The Agency maintains a register open to the public, containing copies of applications, as well as subsequent events such as variations, revocations and prosecutions, but excluding commercially confidential or national-security-sensitive information.

The Agency sends copies of the application to the Health and Safety Executive, the relevant local authority and other statutory consultees.

The Agency must consider any representations made to it. It must determine the application within four months of receipt, otherwise the applicant may take failure to do so as a "deemed refusal" and appeal to the Secretary of State; he may similarly appeal against an actual refusal to grant an authorisation.

Entities

The government's integrated Environment Agency, established by the EA 1995, began to operate on 1 April 1996. It is a non-departmental body corporate, bringing together the powers of Her Majesty's Inspectorate of Pollution, the National Rivers Authority and the waste regulation functions of local authorities. Its principal aim is to protect or enhance the environment so as to contribute to achieving sustainable development. Its powers and duties include pollution control and promotion of conservation, and ministerial guidance will be important in defining these. Its responsibilities include regulation of the most polluting industrial processes (under the IPC regime of the EPA 1990) and of radioactive materials, control of waste and aspects of contaminated land, administering consents to discharge into water, water purity standards and measures to combat water pollution, research, monitoring, reporting and provision of environmental information.

The Health and Safety Executive

This body corporate administers and enforces the controls under the Health and Safety at Work etc. Act 1974 dealing with air pollution and health and safety concerning places at work. It is consulted under the IPC regime of the EPA 1990.

Local authorities

These locally elected bodies have wide-ranging responsibilities for their localities. For environmental matters these include control of air quality, administration of aspects of contaminated land, statutory nuisances and noise, as well as planning and public health.

Time Periods

The statutory period for the authorities to consider an application for authorisation is four months in the case of IPC, local authority air pollution control and waste disposal licences and two months in the case of consent to discharge to water.

Enforcement of Environmental Regulations

National

Enforcement is generally considered to be the task of regulatory authorities aimed at compliance. This has been by a mixture of the persuasive and the punitive approaches. The persuasive approach, criticised as lax and favouring industry, became less so after the Water Act 1989 and EPA 1990 regimes arrived. It has, however, been buttressed by the deregulatory approach being developed under the Deregulation and Contracting Out Act 1994 (which enables enforcement procedures to be varied by ministerial direction and which is, for example, reflected in the Agency's enforcement policies). The punitive approach can involve the use of criminal prosecution for breach of statutes or regulations (see under the legal processes described below), revocation of authorisations, enforcement or prohibition notices, abatement or remediation notices and exercise of the broad and severe powers of inspectors. In taking this approach, especially the use of prosecutions, the authorities exercise discretion and have generally adopted it as a last resort. There have been some successes, *e.g.* the fall in number of serious water pollution incidents. However, enforcement, both persuasive and punitive, has been adversely affected to varying degrees by a lack of uniformity and of predictability in approach, by administrative dislocation and by problems of staffing and funding.

The Agency, the most important instrument of enforcement,

published its principles of enforcement in May 1996. These are in particular:

- proportionality – enforcement action should be proportionate to risks to the environment and to the seriousness of any breach of the law or relevant licence and consent;
- consistency – in advice given, in use of powers, in response to pollution incidents and in decisions on whether to prosecute;
- targeting – directing enforcement action primarily at activities causing the most serious environmental risk or damage; and
- transparency – helping those subject to enforcement action to understand what is expected of them and what they should expect from the Agency.

Save in cases requiring immediate action, the Agency should give notice of its proposed enforcement measures, and those notified are to have the opportunity to make representations against the proposed measures.

The legal processes of enforcement are essentially by the creation and pursuit of criminal and civil liabilities, adjudicated upon by the criminal and civil courts respectively; a separate tribunal to deal with all environmental issues has been suggested. Broadly speaking, environmental statutes provide for criminal and the common law for civil liabilities. The criminal liabilities can often arise even in the absence of guilty intent, and the civil liabilities can arise even in the absence of fault. The liabilities fall on those persons or entities in breach, with the important additional criminal liability under a number of environmental statutes that falls on officers or actively controlling shareholders of companies who had consented to or been negligently involved in the commission of offences by their companies.

It is the designated authorities (the Agency, the Health and Safety Executive and local authorities) that bring criminal prosecutions or actions for recovery of cost of anti-pollution measures (*e.g.* under the WRA 1991).

Pressure groups have instigated action by the European Commission, private prosecutions and judicial review of the enforcement policies of regulatory authorities, and the courts have accepted a broader role for such groups. However, they have no general right to bring civil actions for breaches of environmental law: this is restricted to those individuals or entities who are directly affected by the breaches.

Individuals and companies may bring private prosecutions for breaches of environmental statutes, but more usually they bring actions in the civil courts on the basis of the common law torts, such as nuisance or negligence.

Breach of environmental statutes does not usually by itself give a right to bring a civil action, nor can individuals or companies generally ask the courts to force the designated authorities to take action to enforce environmental statutes.

Civil litigation claiming damages or an injunction as well as judicial review of administrative decisions is becoming increasingly frequent and important: awards of damages and costs of litigation can be large, a number of mass "toxic tort" actions have been brought and some very significant court decisions have been made (*e.g.* on foreseeability of damages in common law tort claims). Individuals and companies are becoming more aware of their rights and have available to them more information about the environment on which to bring civil action to protect their rights.

The authorities mentioned (save for local authorities) and the court systems operate uniformly throughout England and Wales.

Local

The national authorities and court systems have regional or more local establishments, *e.g.*:

- The Agency operates through eight regions: Anglian, Southern, North East, South West, North West, Thames, Midland and Welsh.
- Of the civil courts, the High Court is located in London and has some 130 district registries; at a lower level there are some 240 County Courts located in counties throughout England and Wales.
- Of the criminal courts, there are some 90 Crown Courts located in centres throughout England and Wales; at a lower level there are Magistrates' Courts in communities of any size.
- The appellate courts for both civil and criminal matters are located in London.

Local authorities exercise their powers strictly over their own areas.

Freedom of Access by the Public to Information on the Environment

Essentially, access by the public to information on the environment enables public rights to be more effectively monitored and enforced.

Public registers under the more recent environmental statutes contain a wide range of information, often subject to exemptions for national security, commercial confidentiality and legal proceedings:

- under the EPA 1990: waste management licence applications, convictions for offences, etc.:
- under the EPA 1990: IPC and local authority air pollution control applications and authorisations, revocations, convictions for offences, etc.; this is supplemented by a separate Chemical Releases Inventory;
- under the EPA 1990 (introduced by the EA 1995): contaminated land remediation notices, convictions for offences, etc.; and
- under the WRA 1991: discharge applications, consents, etc.

The Environmental Information Regulations 1992 made under the European Communities Act 1972 implement the EC Freedom of Access to Environmental Information Directive 1990. They provide, in addition to the regime of registers, for a general right of access by the public to information on the environment held by government and by public authorities. Mandatory exceptions include information disclosed voluntarily by a third party and information disclosure of which would increase the likelihood of damage to the environment. Discretionary exceptions include information relating to national security or commercial confidentiality. Information is also made available to the public in the planning process and in the process of environmental assessment of proposed developments. The latter process was formally established by the EC Directive on the Assessment of the Effects of

Certain Private and Public Projects on the Environment 1985. The directive was implemented by the Town and Country Planning (Assessment of Environmental Effects) Regulations 1988, made under the European Communities Act 1972. Certain development projects (*e.g.* chemical installations, thermal power stations) require an assessment; other (*e.g.* for glass or paper manufacture) require an assessment only where they are likely to have a significant environmental effect. The essence of the assessment is the environmental statement prepared by the developer and consultation with statutory and non-statutory consultees, which could include local groups and members of the public.

Environmental Management

The British Standards Institute launched BS7750, the world's first standard on environmental management systems, in 1992. BS7750 is a generic, pro-active, on-going, voluntary, systems-based certification scheme, aiming to be "a foundation for both sound environmental performance and participation in 'environmental auditing' schemes". A participating organisation needs to carry out a review, formulate policy, put in place organisation, personnel and relevant registers, set objectives and targets, engage in a management programme, prepare manuals, documentation and records, set up operational control and undertake a management audit and review – thus setting the process in motion again. BS7750 does not set performance requirements, nor does it confer immunity from the need to comply with legal obligations.

More recent activity has focused on two other systems and the establishment of operational mechanisms. One system is the EC Eco-Management and Audit Scheme (EMAS) Regulation; accreditation by the UK Accreditation Service of verifiers under EMAS has been established, and the relationship of BS7750 to EMAS considered. The other system is the International Standard ISO 14001, which may come to replace BS7750 altogether, or to some extent.

Economic Instruments

Economic incentives and deterrents have included:

- charges for the cost of operating regulatory schemes, *e.g.* charges on IPC applications for authorisations to operate and for operating under the EPA 1990;
- charges on polluting materials, *e.g.* the landfill tax: levied on the disposal of waste to landfill from 1 October 1996, calculated on some categories of waste at a rate lower than the standard rate, with other categories exempt; and payable by the operator of the landfill site (who may obtain a credit if he makes payment to a trust whose object is environmental protection and research);
- reduced charges for less polluting materials, *e.g.* the tax differential in favour of unleaded petrol;
- recycling credits under the EPA 1990 to waste disposal and collection authorities for waste removed from the waste stream for recycling, the credits to reflect savings in disposal and collection costs; and
- government support by grants, *e.g.* for energy from waste schemes and for industrial research into recycling, emissions to the atmosphere, industrial waste treatments, cleaner technology and environmental monitoring; the research grants operate under various schemes.

Major Environmental Initiatives and Pending Proposals

Implementation of new regimes

Implementation of the regimes introduced by the EA 1995, especially the ones concerning national air quality, contaminated land and packaging waste, is a complex and significant task. The operation of the new Agency will be the subject of particular scrutiny.

Consumer Information

The government intends to promote ways in which consumers can make their views known (through a Consumer Environment Forum) and in which information is provided to consumers (by labelling schemes and by more closely controlled environmental claims by manufacturers, primarily through codes of practice).

Transport

The growing concern over transport policy and related issues is set to produce measures which will affect businesses. Measures may include a shift from road building to support for rail and shipping, as well as fiscal mechanisms aimed at promoting public transport and at curbing use of and pollution from road vehicles.

Labour Party Proposals

There will be a general election in the UK before 1998. The Labour Party has published its environmental manifesto, "In Trust for Tomorrow". Its proposals include:

- a contaminated land clean-up initiative, with a tax on pollution to fund clean-up by the authorities;
- legally enforceable environmental rights to clean air, clean drinking water, environmental information, consultation on environmental issues locally and in the place of employment and compensation for environmental damage;
- protection for "whistle-blowers" who disclose breaches of environmental regulation by their employers;
- reporting requirements on larger companies about environmental performance;
- an Environmental Ombudsman who could investigate companies; and
- an environmental division of the High Court to deal with all environmental cases arising under specified acts.

Chapter 6
Environmental Regulation in France

Alex Dowding
Baker & McKenzie, Paris

Sources of Environmental Regulation

In contrast to the Single European Act, the French Constitution contains no reference to environmental policy. Such absence is not surprising, considering that the constitution was adopted in 1958, when environmental considerations were not viewed as fundamental. From a practical standpoint, French environmental regulation is principally passed on a national level by means of laws (*lois*), decrees (*décrets*), orders (*arrêtés*) and circulars (*circulaires*).

The principal initiator of such regulation is the Ministry of the Environment, which defines the government's environmental policy on behalf of and under the authority of the Prime Minister. Other sources of regulation are to be found in a variety of codes (such as the Rural, Public Health and Criminal Codes) which contain certain provisions regarding the environment. An Environment Code is currently in preparation, aiming at harmonising existing environmental legislation and assembling it into one legislative act.

As in the case of a number of other European Community (EC) member states, partial or non-implementation of EC directives has led to enforcement proceedings by the EC Commission against France in the European Court of Justice. A number of such proceedings are because of implementation of directives by the French authorities by means of circulars, which are considered by the EC Commission not to be satisfactorily binding regulations but merely administrative interpretations given by the French central authorities to the local authorities, who are routinely called upon to apply environmental regulations.

Specific Provisions Constituting Environmental Regulation

Air Quality

A number of laws refer indirectly to the prevention of air pollution, in particular the Law on Classified Installations for the Purpose of Environmental Protection (*Installations Classées pour la Protection de l'Environnement*) of 19 July 1976. On 1 March 1993 the Air-Water Integrated Order (*Arrêté Intégré Air/Eau*), in line with the EC Integrated Pollution Prevention Programme, was adopted. It fixes on a national level the maximum acceptable content of each substance in air emissions and water effluent from classified installations subject to an authorisation procedure. The defined levels differ according to the activities concerned. Certain more polluting activities are excluded from this general text, which became effective in April 1994.

The principal air pollution control legislation is the Law of 10 March 1948 on the Use of Energy and the Law of 2 August 1961 on Air Pollution, specifically aimed at controlling airborne emissions from stationary incineration, combustion or heating plants. Implementing decrees, principally the Decree of 13 May 1974 concerning the control of pollution emissions, set the technical compliance specifications.

A draft bill on air and the rational use of energy is being discussed before Parliament and the Senate. It is expected to be adopted in the autumn of 1996 and, with limited exceptions, will replace the 1948 and 1961 laws. The draft bill seeks to impose on the state increased air surveillance and information obligations as well as the implementation of regional plans on the quality of air and plans for the protection of the atmosphere. The interconnection between urban transportation and the environment is also specifically covered by the draft bill, together with other technical and financial aspects and increased sanctions.

The two principal authorities having competence over air pollution are: the DRIRE (*Direction Régionale de l'Industrie, de la Recherche et de l'Environnement*), which monitors classified installations; and the ADEME (*Agence de l'Environnement et de la Maîtrise de l'Energie*). The ADEME monitors emissions, gives technical advice to industry, develops more effective and energy-efficient processes and grants loans and subsidies with the proceeds of a special tax on air emissions. This tax, which has been in existence since 1985, was amended in 1996 to provide for an annual tax of 180FF per tonne to be paid by certain facilities over a certain power (20 megawatts) incinerating household waste or producing over 150 tonnes annually of either sulphur dioxide, nitrogen oxide, hydrochloric acids, non-methanine hydrocarbons, solvents or other VOCs.

Special tax incentives exist to encourage investments in anti-pollution devices in the form of accelerated depreciation of anti-pollution equipment or electric vehicles.

Two important decrees were adopted in February 1996 to set rules for the protection of health against the risks of exposure to asbestos of the general population and workers respectively. In addition, in July 1996 the Ministry of Social Affairs and Labour announced the outright banning (with certain exceptions) of asbestos as from 1 January 1997.

Water Quality

Water quality legislation is characterised by a complex inter-mingling of different pieces of legislation. Until the beginning of 1992, the principal legislation was the Water Law of 16 December 1964 and its main implementing Decree of 23 February 1973, which separates France into six regions and establishes a river basin agency in each region to help control discharges into water-ways and use of water. Funding of regional agencies comes from the proceeds of a water use tax imposed on those drawing on the public water supply, mainly for industrial use and/or discharging into the waterways. The river basin agencies use the tax monies in the form of grants, subsidies and low interest loans to finance pollution reduction technologies.

The 1964 Water Law also provides for water police to control effluent discharges into waterways. All effluent discharges into waterways must be specifically authorised. Generally the authorities take into account the existing level of pollution of the receiving waterways, their use and their capacity to regenerate themselves naturally. Maximum pollution levels are imposed on classified installations.

The Law of 3 January 1992 on Water substantially amended the 1964 Water Law by establishing new management structures for water distribution and increasing sanctions against polluters. The principal novelty of the 1992 law results from the establishment of "integrated planning and management schemes" (*Schémas directeurs d'aménagement et de gestion des eaux* (SDAGE) and *Schémas d'aménagement et de gestion des eaux* (SAGE)). These schemes, at the level of each river basin or group of basins, fix the water management objectives in consultation with regional authorities and interested parties. In addition, water policing has been substantially reinforced and rendered more homogenous, with specific criminal sanctions for pollution provided in the form of increased penalties and/or imprisonment. The law also provides in certain circumstances for declaration or authorisation procedures, both for drawing water and emitting waste effluent into underground or surface water, and provides for improved coordination with the Law of 19 July 1976 on Classified Installations which, in fact, exclusively applies to industrial sites. In this respect, the Integrated Order of 1 March 1993 (see above under Air Quality) fixes the maximum acceptable content of water effluent originating from sites subject to an authorisation procedure.

Noise Pollution

Most significant is the Law of 19 July 1976 on Classified Installations and more specifically an implementing Order of 20 August 1985, as amended by the Integrated Order of 1 March 1993, whereby such installations are compelled to satisfy certain pre-set noise standards. Failure to do so may result in sanctions.

In addition, on 31 December 1992 a comprehensive law on noise abatement was adopted. The text is subject to a number of implementing decrees. It introduces an airport tax to permit the indemnification of residents in the vicinity of airports and adjusts the level of minimum criminal sanctions to imprisonment for up to two years and/or 200,000FF in fines.

Waste Generation

The principal legislation is the Law of 15 July 1975 as amended on Waste Disposal and Material Recovery, which implements the EC Directive on Waste of the same date. The 1975 law covers the disposal of most types of waste and the range of activities associated with this, including collection, transportation, storage, sorting, treatment, dumping and discharge into the environment. The principal enforcement authorities are the DRIRE.

A general obligation imposed by the 1975 law on generators or holders of waste is to ensure disposal in such a way as not to cause a threat to the environment. The disposal mechanism must also seek to facilitate the recovery of materials and energy.

These obligations represent the basis of potential liability for waste generators, who must be able to prove the final destination of their waste shipments. The Law of 19 July 1976 on Classified Installations integrates the generation and elimination of waste into the permitting structure. In fact, certain waste disposal plants are themselves classified installations. Generators, transporters, importers, exporters and disposers of certain toxic industrial waste are also required to provide specific information to the authorities and maintain registers of activity involving waste. A manifest system is also mandated to enable the authorities to control the disposal process of listed substances.

A law of 13 July 1992 substantially amended the 1975 and 1976 laws by providing for the preparation of elimination plans at a regional and departmental level for household and industrial waste.

As for waste disposal sites, the July 1992 law also provides that from July 2002 only "ultimate waste" will be acceptable at waste disposal sites, *i.e.* waste which so far as economically and technically possible has had its recoverable portion extracted and its dangerous characteristics minimised.

The July 1992 law also introduces a landfill tax of 30FF tonne in 1996 (40FF from 1998 until 2002) on all household and assimilated industrial waste, the proceeds of which will normally be used to finance the development and adoption of new treatment technologies and the clean-up of household waste disposal sites. The law also reinforces the control of waste disposal sites and their operators by imposing prior authorisations for sales of such sites and imposing financial guarantees to ensure the satisfactory rehabilitation of the sites after use.

A major innovation of the July 1992 law concerns the sale of land. Under the terms of the law, the vendor of land on which a classified installation subject to an authorisation procedure is operated must inform the purchaser of any important dangers or inconveniences of which he may have knowledge. Failure to do so may enable the purchaser to cancel the sale, obtain a partial refund of the purchase price or request the clean-up of the land sold at the vendor's expense if the cost of such clean-up is not disproportionate to the purchase price.

The July 1992 law also substantially increases the minimum liability of operators of industrial plants for violations of the law on waste (fines from 2,000FF to 5,000,000FF and imprisonment from ten days to six months).

In 1995 a tax on special industrial waste was introduced, the proceeds of which are to be used for the rehabilitation of orphan sites. This tax levies the same amounts as the landfill tax.

The government has proceeded with its plan aiming at recycling packaging materials. Since 1 January 1993, all producers and importers of consumer goods must either recover their own packaging materials or contract with an organisation (*Eco-Emballages SA*) which arranges with local authorities and recyclers for the collection, sorting, recovery and/or recycling of packaging materials. Financing of this network is in the form of a contribution based on the volume or weight of the packaging material.

By contracting with *Eco-Emballages SA* companies are entitled to use the green dot logo as used in Germany as proof of their contribution to the system. Failure to comply with the new regulations may result in imprisonment up to two years and/or a fine of 500,000FF.

In addition, a decree governing industrial and commercial packaging waste, which completes the *Eco-Emballages* system, has been in effect for paper and cardboard packaging waste since 22

September 1994, and all other types of packaging waste since 22 July 1995. Producers or holders of industrial or commercial packaging waste must recover such waste or cause it to be recovered by re-use, recycling or any other method aimed at obtaining re-usable materials or energy.

Environmental Permitting Schemes

The Law of 19 July 1976 on Classified Installations, along with a Decree of 21 September 1977 as amended, governs the operation of plants which may represent a nuisance or a danger to their neighbourhood or to general public health and safety. Classified installations appear on a list (*Nomenclature des Installations Classées*) formally composed of some 400 activities. A complete revision of this list distinguishing substances and activities is expected to be finished in 1996. The presence of an industrial activity on this list generally indicates that the plant undertaking such activity is subject to an "authorisation" or "declaration" process, depending on the level of risks the plant may pose to the environment.

The authorisation process consists of a full permitting procedure. This includes the filing of an application with a thorough impact analysis describing the predictable impact of the plant on the local environment (the content of which has been reinforced in February 1993) and a risk analysis describing the potential dangers presented by the plant and planned preventive and emergency measures.

The authorisation or permit is granted in a decentralised manner by means of a prefectural order (*Arrêté Préfectoral d'Autorisation*) after analysis of the application and the results of public and administrative enquiries. Except for waste disposal sites and quarries, authorisations are usually granted for unlimited periods and are transferable. They generally take nine to twelve months to obtain. Waste disposal sites and quarries must also provide financial guarantees which are aimed at ensuring the satisfactory rehabilitation of the sites upon closure or in case of accidental pollution. Each prefectural order contains site-specific technical obligations fixed by classified installation inspectors from the local

DRIRE authorities. These permit obligations generally impose technical operating requirements, leaving to the plant operator the choice of implementation methods to achieve the requirements. The discretion of the prefects has been reduced with the entry into effect of the Air/Water Integrated Order, although they remain entitled to fix more severe acceptable levels of emissions or effluent than those provided in the order.

The declaration procedure applies to plants that present a lower risk to the environment. Prior to commencing operation, these plants are required to file a declaration with the local prefectural authorities. The plant activities covered by the declaration procedure must be conducted according to standard technical requirements fixed in a model order (*arrêtés-types*). The latter will be progressively reviewed to adapt to the forthcoming changes to the list of activities.

Strict provisions, tantamount to a departure impact analysis, are imposed on sites which are closed. Such sites must be left in a state such that they do not present any nuisance or danger to the environment. The DRIRE has over the last few years been instructed to ensure full compliance with these provisions.

A Ministry of the Environment circular to the competent local authorities (*préfects*) in April 1996 instructs them to initiate soil surveys of industrial sites in their region. The choice of the sites for such a survey is to be determined by the local authorities, based on the deemed risk of pollution associated with the activities. A diagnosis and evaluation obligation will be imposed on the site operators by a distinct prefectural order. The surveys will need to be completed within three to five years, depending on the priority level. The soil survey is also recommended when modifications or extensions of activity are declared by priority sector sites.

Enforcement of Environmental Regulation

The enforcement of environmental regulation is to a large degree in the hands of the classified installations inspectors at the initial stages. Liability resulting from violations of environmental regulations and/or environmentally related damage to third parties may take one of the following three forms:

Administrative Sanctions

If an installation is operated without prior authorisation or without filing the proper declaration, the prefect may require the plant operator to fulfil the operating obligations or even close down the plant.

If the applicable technical requirements are not complied with, the prefect may carry out the necessary work to put the plant into compliance at the operator's expense and/or order the operator to pay an amount corresponding to the cost of the work to be performed. Closure of the plant may also be ordered.

All such prefectural orders may be contested before the administrative courts. In the case of a plant closure, the operator's obligation to continue paying its employees is provided by law.

From a practical standpoint it is the administrative liability which presents the most risks and which is the most commonly applied. Such liability is also characterised by the absence of any statute of limitations.

Criminal Sanctions

In the circumstances of administrative liability set out above, the plant managers, company presidents, managers or general managers, and eventually certain of the company's employees, may incur criminal sanctions including fines up to 500,000FF and up to one year's imprisonment for first offences, and 1,000,000FF and two years' imprisonment for subsequent offences. To escape liability for such sanctions a formal delegation of powers to the employee concerned must be demonstrated. The court will also verify whether the employee effectively has the necessary authority, competence and means to act. Indeed, a delegation of powers may not always suffice to exonerate fully a company president or manager if he can be considered to have contributed to the offence (*e.g.* not providing the employee with sufficient financial resources to comply with the law).

The criminal court may also close down the plant or order the operator to take remedial steps within a set period. Traditionally, a criminal offence must be characterised by three elements: a legal, a material and a moral element; however, in the environmental field, the moral element (*i.e.* intentional element, the consciousness of the illegality of the act or omission) tends to be more limited than for other types of criminal liability.

A major development having far-reaching effects in the environmental sector has been the implementation of the criminal responsibility of corporate entities.

Since March 1994, companies and other legally recognised entities, including foreign companies, committing criminal offences may be directly pursued by the Public Prosecutor for an extensive number of crimes, misdemeanours and offences.

Acts committed by the companies' management bodies or their representatives, such as acts of negligence or imprudence and negligence or non-compliance with safety obligations causing death or bodily injury are covered under the new Penal Code.

The criminal liability of the company does not exclude or replace the personal liability of the individuals who committed the offence. The penalties provided include the creation of a "criminal record" for convicted companies, fines (which may be up to five times those imposed on individuals), limitations on the right to perform certain activities (*e.g.* the raising of public funds), exclusions from public tenders, temporary or permanent prohibitions to conduct certain activities, judicial scrutiny, temporary or permanent cessation of business operations, the confiscation of the asset contributing to the offence or the product thereof, and even the dissolution of the company.

As for the statute of limitations applicable to criminal liability, the Public Prosecutor may trigger criminal proceedings against a person or entity for as long as the sanctioned action or omission continues. Therefore, the statute of limitations (one and three years, depending on the offence) will only commence once the violation has formally ceased. A civil action for damages may be commenced before the criminal court for as long as the action of the Public Prosecutor is not statute-barred.

Civil Liability

There are no specific civil liability rules applicable to the environmental sector. Common law tort principles are therefore applied, the person or entity having caused the damage being therefore liable to repair it. The concept of punitive damages does not exist.

Compliance with existing regulations does not exonerate the plant operator, since all operating permits are granted subject to the rights of third parties.

Any third party who suffers damage may bring a court action against the plant operator. As nobody is authorised to claim to represent the public interest, non-profit organisations wishing to file an environmental claim must at least be able to demonstrate having suffered some direct or indirect prejudice.

The straightforward application of common law tort principles has been modified by the tendency of the courts to apply *de facto* in the environmental field a concept of strict liability, even though the applicable tort statute may require the demonstration of fault. This tendency, frequently based on the so-called "abnormal neighbourhood inconvenience", may be paving the way to the concept of objective liability. France has, however, yet to sign the Lugano Convention on civil liability for damage resulting from activities dangerous for the environment.

A civil liability claim may also be based on the concept of deemed control of the relevant persons or elements (*e.g.* of the toxic air emissions causing the damage). Such a tort concept also dispenses with the need for the plaintiff to prove fault. In the case of a number of persons or entities responsible, any one can be called upon to pay the full damages, subject to his right then to take action against the other defendants.

The statute of limitations before the civil courts in tort is ten years from the manifestation or aggravation of the damage.

Traditionally, insurance coverage for environmental civil liability damage came under companies' general liability policies and fire and explosion policies. With time, French insurance companies have tended to exclude or severely restrict pollution risks from such policies. Such risks may now be covered by a pollution pool (ASSURPOL) which provides pollution insurance. ASSURPOL currently covers up to 192 million francs per loss per year of insurance. The standard ASSURPOL contract, however, contains numerous exclusions.

Availability of Information on the Environment

A law of 17 July 1978 and its implementing decree of 18 November 1983 set out the general principle of free access to general administrative documentation. This legislation is completed by a law of 12 July 1983 on the democratisation of public enquiries and the protection of the environment and by a law of 30 December 1988 which acknowledges the right of any person to be informed of the negative effects on human health and the environment resulting from the collection, transport and storage of waste, as well as the steps taken to prevent or neutralise such effects. A law of 22 July 1987 concerning the organisation of the *"sécurité civile"* ("public safety authority") also acknowledges citizens' rights to information on major technological or natural risks to which they may be exposed.

These internal provisions may need to be completed by legislation required to implement fully the 1990 EC Directive on Freedom of Access to Environmental Information.

Environmental Trends

The next few years should be characterised by a general reinforcement of environmental regulations in France, partially as a result of the continued implementation of EC Directives. Taxes applicable to "polluters" are scheduled to increase progressively and their scope will be widened (air tax, taxes on ordinary and special industrial waste, taxes on water effluent, etc.).

The preparation of the Environmental Code is moving forward, the legislative section (comprising 858 articles) was submitted to the government in February 1996 and the regulatory section is expected to be completed by the end of 1996.

The new air law is expected to be adopted in the autumn of 1996.

France

The Minister of Environment has, however, indicated her intent to slow down the legislative process, namely legislation originating from the European institutions, which has severely reinforced the legislation applicable to industry. It appears that such expression of intent is rather unlikely to be implemented, considering the ever-increasing consumer pressures in the environmental field throughout Europe.

Chapter 7
Environmental Regulation in the Federal Republic of Germany

Joachim Scherer*
Baker & McKenzie, Frankfurt/Main

Regulatory and Organisational Framework

In the Federal Republic of Germany (FRG) the protection of the environment remains one of the prime concerns of policy makers, the business community and the public at large.

Sources of Environmental Regulation

The regulatory instruments include federal and state laws (*Gesetze*) and ordinances based on these and having the effect of law (*Rechtsverordnung*). Such ordinances may be issued by the federal government, a federal minister, the state governments or a state minister.

Of particular importance are administrative rules (*Verwaltungsvorschriften*) adopted by federal or state administrative authorities. They are used as guidelines for the exercise of discretionary powers, as interpretations of the law and to establish pollution standards, measuring methods and pollution control instruments. Local byelaws (*Satzungen*) are another source of environmental law at the local and regional levels. Such byelaws, which require express statutory authorisation, may govern, *inter alia*, the disposal

*The author gratefully acknowledges the assistance of Ulrich Ellinghaus (Baker & McKenzie, Frankfurt) in the preparation of this chapter.

of waste by local waste disposal entities, the conditions of use of local or regional waste dumps, and the discharge of water into local waste water purification systems.

Division of Federal and State Powers

The legislative powers in the field of environmental law are divided under the Federal Constitution (the "Basic Law" – *Grundgesetz* (GG)) between the federation (*Bund*) and the federal states (*Laender*).

Under the GG, the *Bund* has concurrent legislative powers and thus can pre-empt the *Laender* legislation in several areas of environmental law, including waste disposal, pollution control and hazardous substances legislation. In areas of nature protection and water resources management, the *Bund* merely has the right to enact framework laws (*Rahmengesetze*), which are complemented and implemented by more detailed *Laender* laws.

Federalism also characterises the exercise of executive powers in the field of environmental law. Whereas environmental legislation is primarily enacted on the federal level, executive competence rests largely with the *Laender* and their administrative entities (districts, counties, and communes).

Environmental Authorities

Because of the distribution of executive powers, the *Bund* has few administrative authorities in the environmental field; they include the Federal Minister for the Environment, the Federal Environmental Office, the Federal Health Office and the Federal Office for Nature Conservation.

The jurisdiction of the environmental and health/industrial safety regulatory agencies on the *Laender* level is defined on the basis of general organisational rules of federal and state laws and/ or the specific provisions organised into three tiers (superior, upper and lower state authorities). The superior state authorities are the State Ministers of Environmental Affairs. Their task is to partici-pate – through ministerial working groups together with the

Federal Ministry of the Environment – in the drafting of environmental laws and ordinances, to supervise the execution of
environmental laws and to take decisions in individual cases
of political importance. The upper state authorities are, in general,
the district administrations or district presidents (*Bezirks-
regierung/Regierungspräsident*). They are subject to administrative
rulings from the superior state authority and, in turn, supervise
the lower state authorities. The lower state authorities are part
of the county or city administrations, implementing environmental
laws at the local level.

Environmental Law in East Germany

The greatest challenge of German environmental policy and law
for the decades to come is the improvement of environmental
conditions in the former German Democratic Republic (GDR)
and the establishment of environmental administrations in the
East German states of Brandenburg, Mecklenburg-Vorpommern,
Saxony, Saxony-Anhalt, Thuringia and Berlin (unified with the
western part of the city to form the State of Berlin). These new
states became part of the FRG on 3 October 1990, and the GDR
ceased to exist. The environmental laws of the GDR have almost
completely been replaced by those of the FRG and the new federal
states.

Specific Provisions, Statutes and Regulations Applicable to Certain Areas of Environmental Regulation

Air Quality/Industrial Hazards

The most important body of law is the Federal Emission Control
Act (*Bundes-Immmissionsschutzgesetz* (BImSchG)), which is complemented by 21 federal ordinances and numerous administrative
rules.

The regulatory approach of the BImSchG is:

91

- installation oriented: the BImSchG governs the establishment and operation of certain stationary emission sources;
- product oriented: the BImSchG governs the emission-related performance standards and quality features of installations, substances and products, including fuel oil and fuels;
- traffic oriented: the BImSchG establishes basic requirements for the performance and operation of vehicles and for the establishment of roads and railways; and
- region oriented: the BImSchG establishes a system of supervision and reduction of air pollution in highly polluted and "smog" areas.

One of the key elements of the regulatory scheme under the BImSchG is the term "harmful environmental impacts", which is defined as "emissions which, according to their type, scope or duration, may cause dangers, substantial disadvantages or nuisances for the public or the neighbourhood". The term "emissions" is defined as "air pollution, sounds, vibrations, light, heat, rays and similar environmental impacts, which affect human beings, animals, plants or other tangibles". "Air pollution" is defined as "alteration of the natural composition of the air".

Limit values for emissions are established by the Technical Instruction on Air, an administrative rule. Air pollution from harmful substances such as lead, cadmium, sulphur dioxide and others is restricted by special federal ordinances under the BImSchG.

The regulatory system of the BImSchG contains a fundamental distinction between installations which require a permit and those which do not but are subject to specific operating requirements. The term "installation" is defined to include factories, plants and other stationary facilities, machines, implements and any other moveable technical facilities and real property on which substances are stored or disposed of or where works which may create emissions are being performed. Installations which require a permit are exhaustively listed in an ordinance, by industry sectors.

Certain installations require a formal permit procedure, including public notice and a hearing. A simplified permit procedure applies to specific types of installations, which by the scope of their nature or by their production are less likely to generate hazardous emissions.

If the permit requirements in the BImSchG, the implementing ordinances and other provisions of public law are met and if the relevant industrial safety concerns are complied with, the administrative authority is required to grant the permit. The permit may be granted subject to specific obligations and conditions, so far as necessary to ensure that the permit requirements will be met. Permit decisions are subject to review by the administrative courts.

In 1995, the BImSchG was to provide for restrictions and prohibitions of road traffic in certain areas in case of smog. Driving a vehicle without a catalitic converter is prohibited when ozone levels reach 240 microgrammes/m³ and the same ozone concentrations are expected for the next day. The prohibition does not apply, *inter alia*, to public transportation and to commuters.

Partly as a consequence of the accident in the chemical factory at Seveso and in implementation of a corresponding EC directive, the federal government adopted an ordinance on the basis of the BImSchG for the prevention of accidents from large industrial installations (Disruptive Events Ordinance – *Störfallverordnung*). This ordinance was substantially revised in 1991 and lays down strict safety standards for the operation of industrial installations likely to cause hazards in the case of accidents. The operations of most installations requiring a permit are subject to specific safety, record-keeping, notification and emergency requirements if certain toxic, flammable, explosive or other hazardous substances are used. In particular, operators are required to submit to the authorities a safety analysis and detailed inventories of hazardous substances which are stored on the site. Furthermore, all disruptive events and even mere disturbances of regular operations which could cause damage to the public or to the neighbourhood must be reported to the authorities. Operators of relevant installations are obligated to inform neighbours and other persons potentially affected by accidents of the safety measures to be taken in the case of accidents and to coordinate these measures with the competent authorities.

Water Management

The Regulatory Framework

Water resources management is governed, in essence, by:

- the Federal Water Management Act (*Wasserhaushaltsgesetz* (WHG));
- the State Water Acts of the federal states; and
- the Act concerning Waste Water Charges (*Abwasserabgabengesetz*).

Additionally, waste water treatment may be subject to local requirements set forth in municipal byelaws.

The WHG is a framework act, supplemented by the State Water Acts. Most of the WHG provisions, however, are directly applicable in the various states. The WHG applies to surface and coastal water and groundwater. It contains general provisions applicable to all types of waters, in particular the general rule that all measures which may affect waters (including all water use) shall be taken in such a manner as to avoid any negative impact upon water quality and to ensure the economic use of water.

The WHG mandates an authorisation for any use of water. Water use includes: abstraction and diversion of water, damming and lowering of surface water, abstraction of solid substances from surface and groundwater, diversion and discharge of substances into water and generally all measures capable of making permanently or substantially harmful changes to the physical, chemical or biological properties of water.

Use authorisations are granted at the discretion of the competent water authority and may be issued subject to conditions and obligations. Conditions and obligations are permissible, *inter alia*, in order to prevent disadvantageous impact upon third parties or to compensate for such impact.

Surface Water Protection

Among the various uses of surface waters, the discharge of waste water directly into such waters is of particular concern to the legislature and to the regulatory authorities. Under the WHG a permit for discharge of waste water will only be granted if the level of contaminants is kept as low as possible in compliance with certain administrative rules, but at least according to the "generally accepted standards of technology".

The discharge of waste water into public water purification systems is governed by state laws, which generally require a discharge permit. These permits are subject to specific conditions which establish, *inter alia*, minimum quality requirements for the waste water and other physical and chemical parameters.

Groundwater Protection

Uses of groundwater also require an authorisation.

Groundwater is protected under the WHG and by several preventive rules, including detailed provisions governing the establishment and operation of waste water installations, pipeline installations for storing, filling, manufacturing and treating dangerous substances, as well as installations for the commercial and public use of such substances.

These installations must fulfil specific quality requirements and be built, established, maintained and operated in such a manner that water pollution is prevented. They are generally subject to a notification requirement and to a system of quality control based on individual approval or type approval. The operator is obliged to monitor the safety of such installations and to provide for regular inspections by licensed experts.

Several state Water Acts establish reporting requirements if it is suspected that hazardous substances will enter or have entered into surface waters, the soil or the public sewage system.

The requirement is on anyone who operates, maintains, repairs, cleans or inspects the relevant installations.

Liability under the Water Act

The WHG provides for strict (*i.e.* no-fault) liability on the polluter of water and of the operator of certain environmentally relevant installations. Anyone who puts or discharges substances into water or otherwise affects water so as to alter its physical, chemical or biological properties, must pay compensation for any damage caused to third parties.

The operator (*Inhaber*) of installations for the production, processing, storing, disposing, transportation or diversion of substances which are likely to alter the properties of water must pay compensation for damage caused by the entry of substances from such installations into water. The functional description encompasses a variety of stationary and mobile installations, including manufacturing plants, tank storage installations and tank vehicles. The operator is liable for all, even accidental, damage caused, except for damage caused by *force majeure*. The operator is the person having the actual and legal power of disposition over the installation. In the case of lease agreements or company surrender agreements, the person having the right to use the installation is generally considered the operator.

Waste Water Charges Act

The Waste Water Charges Act seeks to create economic incentives to minimise water pollution. The generator of waste water which is discharged directly into surface or groundwater is obliged to pay an annual charge. The revenues so generated are used to improve water quality. The charges are computed in "harmful substance units" on the basis of the harmfulness of the waste water: having regard to the quantity and any specific harmful substances involved.

Waste Management

The Regulatory Framework

Waste management is governed by federal legislation and, to the extent that the federal government has not exercised its legislative powers, by concurrent state legislation.

The centerpiece of waste legislation is the Closed Substance

Cycle and Waste Management Act (*Kreislaufwirtschafts- und Abfallgesetz* (KrW-/AbfG)) of September 1994 which in October 1996 replaced the Federal Avoidance and Disposal of Wastes Act of 1986 (*Abfallgesetz*(AbfG)).

The KrW-/AbfG reinforces the priorities of waste avoidance and waste recycling already contained in the Waste Disposal Act. Other than the AbfG, the KrW-/AbfG does not limit itself to the end of the life-span of a product, but establishes a "cradle-to-grave" system of product management which takes into consideration the design of a product as well. A product has to be designed in such a way as to reduce the amount of, and harm from, waste, *e.g.* by allowing for multiple use and harmless disposal. In principle the new act allows for monitoring the effects of a product on waste avoidance and reduction during the whole life-span of the product.

The new act establishes a hierarchy of waste avoidance, re-use and disposal. Residues must be avoided; if they cannot be avoided, they must be re-used either through recycling or through incineration; only as a last resort may residues be disposed of as waste.

Key elements of the new act are:

- the obligation of industry to avoid residues; and
- the obligation of manufacturers to develop, manufacture and place on the market products that are designed for multiple use and that can be disposed of without harm to the environment.

The obligation to re-use residues as secondary raw materials is subject to technical feasibility and economic reasonableness. Incineration – as one form of re-use of residues as secondary raw materials – is permissible only in narrowly defined circumstances, including compliance with requirements concerning the calorific value of each type of residue.

The KrW-/AbfG will be complemented by several federal ordinances, such as the Ordinance on the Tracking of Waste (*Nachweisverordnung*) and the amended Ordinance on the Avoidance of Packaging Waste (Packaging Ordinance – *Verpackungsverordnung*).

The existing Packaging Ordinance under the *Abfallgesetz* already establishes a comprehensive system of waste management measures with the objective of avoiding waste from packaging materials. The ordinance applies to the manufacturers of pack-aging and to anybody ("distributors") who markets packaging or products from which packaging is directly manufactured or goods in packaging, irrespective of the commercial level on which the transaction occurs. In principle, manufacturers and distributors are obliged to take back used packaging and to provide for its re-use or recycling. Packaging for beverages, washing and cleaning detergents and dispersion paints are subject to mandatory deposit schemes. The obligations to take back, re-use and recycle as well as the deposit schemes do not apply if manufacturers and distributors participate in an approved "collection system" which guarantees a regular collection of used packaging at households or in their vicinity within the "catchment areas" of particular distributors. The objective of this regulatory scheme is to enhance the establish-ment of a "dual" waste disposal system consisting of the (existing) public waste disposal system and a new, secondary waste disposal system which is privately owned and operated on behalf (and at the expense of) those industry sectors which generate packaging waste.

In order to establish such a system in practice, a private company was established in 1990 by a group of companies from the packaging industry and commerce to organise the collection, recovery and recycling of sales packaging returned by the customer (*Duales System Deutschland Gesellschaft für Abfallvermeidung und Sekundärrohstoffgewinnung mbH* – DSD). The DSD itself does not operate any collection and recycling undertakings, but coordinates and supervises their activities. Any producer of pack-aging may take part in the system by making a financial contribution to the DSD, in exchange for which the latter confers the licence to mark the packaging with a "Green Dot", indicating that the packaging may be recycled. The financial contributions of the producers or distributors of packaging serve to set up and operate the necessary collection and recycling facilities.

The essential practical feature of the system is that these under-takings provide special yellow containers or plastic sacks to households. Customers ideally should place all packaging bearing a "Green Dot" in these yellow bins or sacks and no longer in the standard bins set up by the public waste collection undertakings.

The yellow bins and sacks are collected by private undertakings and brought to sorting and recycling facilities.

In order to avoid ordinances promulgating the establishment of take-back obligations for certain types of wastes, German industry has committed itself to reduce voluntarily the amount of waste generated in specific areas. For example, the German car industry has declared its voluntary commitment to reduce the percentage of waste from used cars from the current 25% per car to 15% by 2002 and to 5% by 2015. To avoid waste, most parts of used cars shall be taken back and recycled. To this end, the car industry agreed to establish a system of collection of used cars within the next two years. Cars that are not older than 12 years will be taken back at no cost. As for electronic waste an ordinance is under active consideration, although the government favours a voluntary commitment by industry.

Waste Disposal

Waste disposal is a "public task" which is discharged by public law entities (counties, cities, etc.) designated by the state waste laws. The waste disposal entities may exclude certain wastes from the public waste disposal system if such wastes cannot be disposed of together with household wastes because of their type or their quantity. These "special wastes" (*Sonderabfälle*), which may comprise industrial wastes and rubble, must then be disposed of by the waste generators or on their behalf, either in licensed waste disposal installations operated by the waste generator himself or by waste disposers.

All waste disposers (public entities, waste generators who dispose of their own waste and private waste disposers used by public entities or by private waste generators) are obliged to dispose of waste in such a manner that human health and well-being are not affected, that fauna and flora are not endangered, that waters, soil and plants are not damaged and that public safety and order is not endangered. This basic principle of orderly waste disposal is complemented by the requirement that waste shall only be processed, stored or disposed of in installations or facilities which are licensed for this purpose ("waste disposal installations").

The disposal of hazardous wastes – *i.e.* wastes from commercial or other economic or public enterprises, which because of their type, quality or quantity are explosive, flammable, particularly hazardous to health, to the air or water, or which may contain or generate organisms causing contagious diseases – is subject to specific safety requirements for transportation, storage and disposal.

The Federal Ordinance on the Determination of Waste (*Abfallbestimmungsverordnung*) defines 350 types of waste as "wastes requiring special supervision". These wastes are specified by a precise designation of their properties and constituents, by a description of the processes and activities during which, or the type of business where, they are generated and by a waste code number. For these wastes, the Technical Instruction on Waste (TA-Abfall) establishes mandatory disposal requirements and "disposal paths". For example, paint thinners and solvents must be disposed of in hazardous waste incinerators; galvanisation sludges containing cyanide must be disposed of by chemical and physical treatment; wastes containing arsenic must be deposited in underground waste disposal facilities. Other specific disposal requirements are defined in the Technical Instruction on Household Waste.

The environmental hazards arising from the uncontrolled handling of "residual substances", *i.e.* substances which are designated for recycling, are comparable to the hazards of uncontrolled waste disposal. If "residual substances" were subject to less stringent supervision requirements than waste, both waste generators and waste transporters might have an incentive to circumvent the waste control requirements. In order to prevent this, the Federal Ordinance for the Determination of Residual Substances (*Reststoffbestimmungsverordnung*) contains a list defining "residual substances" in the same manner as the Ordinance on the Determination of Wastes. In fact, the lists are largely identical, because most hazardous wastes can also be recycled. The listed "residual substances" are subject to essentially the same supervision requirements as hazardous wastes. These requirements are set out in the Ordinance on the Collection, Transportation and Supervision of Waste and Residual Substances (*Verordnung über das Einsammeln und Befördern sowie über die Überwachung von*

Abfällen und Reststoffen), which establishes a "cradle-to-grave" system of supervision of the disposal of hazardous wastes and residual substances.

Waste Transportation

For the collection and transportation of waste as a business or the course of business activities (*e.g.* between different plants of the same enterprise) a permit is required. This permit requirement is an integral part of the concept of ensuring the orderly disposal of waste from "cradle-to-grave". Furthermore, the transborder transportation of waste is subject to strict permit and control requirements based on EC law.

Noise Pollution

Noise pollution is governed by the BImSchG and several ordinances concerning specific sources of noise. Maximum levels are provided for in an administrative rule, the Technical Instruction on Noise.

Liability for Historic Contamination: The *"Altlasten"* Problem

Legally and illegally operated waste dumps and the release of hazardous substances by industrial enterprises and public entities have created numerous contaminated sites in Germany. "Historic contamination" (*Altlasten*), *i.e.* soil and/or groundwater contamination resulting from deactivated or abandoned waste disposal sites and from industrial uses, have become a political, economic and legal problem of considerable dimensions. According to realistic estimates, West Germany has some 80,000 suspected old contamination sites. Because of insufficient implementation of environmental laws in the former GDR, the situation in East Germany may be much more serious. Studies suggest that about

60,000 sites are likely to be contaminated. Additionally, most, if not all, of the 750 licensed waste installations and many of the 5,000 "uncontrolled" and 7,500 illegal waste dumps in East Germany will require clean-up.

Under the (GDR) Environmental Framework Act of 1990, the purchasers of industrial installations could apply by 31 December 1991 for an exemption from liability for historic contamination in the former GDR. This deadline was subsequently extended to 28 March 1992. Some 60,000 applications have been filed. In an administrative agreement concluded in the spring of 1993, the federal states and the Federal Privatisation Agency (*Treuhandanstalt*) have agreed in principle on the division of the cost of the remediation of sites for which an exemption has been granted.

The Legal Framework

The assessment, investigation and clean-up of historic contamination is not governed by one single, comprehensive act comparable to the US CERCLA. Rather, historic contamination is subject to numerous federal and state laws, depending upon the time the contamination occurred, the circumstances, the type and the origin of the contamination. As a consequence, each case of historic contamination requires a careful analysis both of the origin of the contamination and the applicable legal framework. Depending upon the circumstances, historic contamination may be subject to waste laws, water protection laws or to the general Police Acts of the federal states. Most federal states have adopted specific acts governing the clean up of historic contaminations. Several state acts provide for public funds in order to pay for decontamination measures where no polluter or other responsible party can be held liable. The Police Acts apply to the extent that no other, more specific law applies. Under these acts the authorities may order investigation and clean-up in any case of danger to public safety and order. As for historic contamination, the legal concept of "danger to public safety and order" encompasses any event, act or omission which endangers human life or health, property, nature, water, soil or other "public property". The

required degree of probability of a danger depends on the seriousness of potential damage: the more serious the likely damage, the
smaller the required degree of probability.

In case of danger to public safety and order, the authority can
take all appropriate preventive measures. The appropriate investigatory and clean-up measures are subject to the principle of
proportionality and determined on a case-by-case basis, depending
upon the type and the scope of the historic contamination, previous and present use and the particular geological and
hydrogeological conditions. Several states have issued recommendations and guidelines for investigatory and clean-up measures.

Under the Police Acts, the authorities may issue orders to the
entity causing the disturbance (*Handlungsstörer*) or responsible
for the condition causing disturbance (*Zustandsstörer*). The entity
causing the disturbance is the entity causing the contamination
("the polluter"), the entity responsible for the disturbing condition
is the owner of the real property from which the danger to public
order and safety emanates, as well as any person (*e.g.* tenant,
lessee) having the actual control over such property ("the user").

In principle, the administrative authorities have a discretion to
hold either the polluter or the user responsible, although court
decisions indicate that the polluter should be held primarily responsible and that contractual agreements between the polluter and
a purchaser (and subsequent user) of contaminated real property
should be taken into consideration. Because of the authorities'
discretion, the purchaser of contaminated real property may be
held liable for historic contamination of such property, even
though caused by previous users. In exercising their discretion the
authorities may also, as confirmed by administrative courts, select
the entity causing the disturbance with the greatest financial
resources. Furthermore, the authorities are not obliged to hold
only one such entity liable but may, at their discretion, hold several
or all such entities liable. The exercise of the administrative discretion is subject to limited court review, in particular with regard to
abuses and excesses of discretionary powers, including violation
of the principle of proportionality.

Indemnification between several polluters – *i.e.* between those
entities causing a disturbance who have been held liable by the
authorities and other entities – is generally not governed by law

(with the exception of Hessen and Rhineland-Palatinate) and should therefore be covered in purchase agreements. Furthermore, the question of legal succession is of crucial importance in cases of historic contamination and must be taken into consideration in all transactions involving potentially contaminated sites and businesses which may have caused such contamination.

It is important to note that neither polluter liability nor user liability is subject to a limitation period.

Hazardous Substances

The protection of people and the environment from risks represented by hazardous substances is one of the priorities of German environmental policy. The basic policy approach is to determine the hazardous properties of a given substance and to classify, label, restrict or prohibit the substance, depending upon the degree of hazard presented by it. Ideally, the risk assessment of hazardous substances should be carried out as a preventive measure before they are put on the market.

Hazardous substances legislation is substantially influenced by EC directives. The general framework of hazardous substances regulation is provided by the Chemicals Act (*Chemikaliengesetz* (ChemG)). The act was intended as a comprehensive statute governing hazardous substances. However, in part because of poor drafting of the ChemG, in part because of the complexity of the effects of hazardous substances, legislation governing hazardous substances has remained extremely complex and is still far from being a coherent statutory scheme. The ChemG is implemented by several federal ordinances, in particular the Ordinance on Hazardous Substances (*Gefahrstoffverordnung* (GefStoffV)).

Specific hazardous substances provisions are also contained in specific statutes, such as the Plant Varieties Protection Act (*Pflanzenschutzgesetz*) governing the use of pesticides, and the Drug Act (*Arzneimittelgesetz*).

Safety standards for the transportation of hazardous goods, including hazardous substances, are established on the basis of the Act on the Transportation of Hazardous Goods (*Gesetz über die*

Beförderung gefährlicher Güter) and the implementing ordinances governing transportation by rail, road and boat.

Objectives and Regulatory Instruments of the ChemG

The objective of the ChemG is to protect people and the environment from the harmful effects of hazardous substances. The act pursues this objective by establishing essentially three regulatory instruments:

- A registration procedure for new chemical substances prior to their manufacture, importation or marketing. As for the registration and testing requirements, the ChemG distinguishes between new and "old" substances. "Old" substances are those (approximately 100,100) substances which were on the market in the EC between 1 January 1971 and 18 September 1981. These substances are listed in the European Inventory of Existing Commercial Chemical Substances (EINECS). The EINECS has been implemented in Germany on the basis of the Old Chemical Substances Ordinance (*Chemikalien-altstoffverordnung*). Any substance which is not listed in the EINECS is subject to the registration procedure.

  Registration of new chemical substances is predicated upon extensive examination of the effects of the new substance upon health and the environment. The manufacturer or importer must submit the examination results to enable the authorities to perform a risk assessment and to decide upon the conditions for manufacturing and marketing. If the applicant is going to market more than one tonne of the new substance per year, the new substance cannot be placed on the market for 60 days after its first registration, subject to extensions in case of additional requests for information. If he plans to market less than one tonne of the new substance, he has to wait for 30 days before marketing the new substance.

  The authority must acknowledge receipt of the registration within 60 and 30 days, respectively. Unless it raises objections to the completeness or correctness of the registration documents, the substance may be put on the market, notwithstanding its hazards, after 60 and 30 days, respectively. If the manufacturer or importer has produced the substance in or imported it from another member state and has registered the substance in an equivalent procedure, the registration procedure is simplified. In particular, the importer or manufacturer does not need to file documents testing on disposal or recycling and neutralisation procedures.

- A system of classification, labelling and packaging of hazardous substances. Hazardous substances are classified either by operation of law or on the basis of self-declaration by the manufacturer or the importer according to hazard criteria defined by statute (*Gefährlichkeitsmerkmale*).
- To the extent that classification, labelling and packaging requirements are not sufficient to prevent damage to life, health and the environment, the federal government is empowered by the ChemG to prohibit or restrict by federal ordinance the manufacture, marketing or use of specific hazardous substances, preparations or products releasing or containing such substances, to establish notification, permit or other requirements for the manufacture, marketing or use of such substances and to prohibit processes of manufacture and use which generate such substances. Since 1993 most prohibitions are contained in two ordinances. Prohibitions concerning chemicals are set out in the Ordinance Concerning the Prohibition of Chemicals (*Chemikalienverbotsverordnung*), while the Hazardous Substances Ordinance prohibits the manufacture and use of certain substances, including asbestos, mercury and its combinations, as well as PCB, PCT, PCP and its combinations.

Hazardous Substances Ordinance

The Hazardous Substances Ordinance contains, *inter alia*, general prohibitions on the classification, packaging and labelling of hazardous substances, general provisions on the handling of hazardous substances, and additional requirements for the handling of carcinogenic or mutagenic substances. The handling of hazardous substances is subject to the industrial hygiene and occupational health requirements set out in the ordinance.

Under the basic principle of the GefStoffV an employer handling hazardous substances must comply with the GefStoffV and its attachments, with sector-specific workplace protection and industrial safety rules and with the generally accepted rules on industrial safety, health and hygiene.

Enforcement of Environmental Regulation

Civil Liability for Environmental Non-Compliance

Personal and corporate civil liabilities for environmental non-compliance may arise as:

- liability to refrain from or to remove interference with the property of another person;
- liability for compensation within a neighbour relationship; and
- liability for damages under tort law and strict liability statutes.

Under the civil law an owner of land is entitled to prohibit the intrusion of gases, vapours, smells, smoke, soot, heat, noise, shocks and similar interference emanating from other land if such interference is material, not in compliance with local customs (*nicht ortsüblich*) and if pollution control measures are economically feasible for the polluter.

If the neighbour is obliged to tolerate intrusions which prejudice the use of or income from his property over and above what may be expected, financial compensation may be payable.

Under tort law any natural or legal person is liable for environmental damage to the extent that it constitutes injury to the life, body, health, freedom, property or other right (such as the right to establish and operate a business) of another person, provided that such injury is unlawful and was caused wilfully or negligently. Wilful or negligent violation of a "protective law" (*Schutzgesetz*) also incurs civil law liability.

Under tort law generally the burden of proof of the wrongful act, the damage and the causation of the damage by the act is on the plaintiff, but the Federal Supreme Court (*Bundesgerichtshof* (BGH)) eased this burden of proof in favour of the plaintiff in the landmark Kupolofen decision. Under this ruling, the plaintiff is merely required to prove that damage was caused by a situation created by the defendant; then it is for the defendant to prove that his emissions were immaterial or in accordance with local custom and that he took all reasonable and economically feasible pollution control measures.

Strict Liability under the Environmental Damage Act

Strict (no-fault) liability for environmental damage has long been limited to the operators of several narrowly defined types of installations and particularly hazardous activities, including water pollution and the operation of certain pipeline installations and of nuclear power installations.

The Environmental Liability Act (*Gesetz über die Umwelthaftung* (UmweltHG)) of 10 December 1989 provides for strict liability of the owners of numerous environmentally relevant installations for damage caused by environmental effects emanating from such installations.

Liability under the UmweltHG is predicated upon the following premises:

- The environmental effects must emanate from one of some 100 types of installations listed in an annexe to the act. The list includes virtually all installations which require a permit under the existing Federal Pollution Control Act, such as furnaces, gas turbines, cooling towers, chemical manufacturing installations and pharmaceutical installations, paint shops, storage facilities for hazardous substances, as well as installations governed by the Waste Management Act.
- Liability is not restricted to operational installations but applies also to "unfinished" and de-activated installations.
- The owner is liable for damage caused by an "environmental effect" emanating from the installation. The requirement of an "environmental effect" is intended to emphasise the ecological objective of strict liability and to restrict its scope. Damage is deemed to have been caused by an environmental effect if caused by substances, vibrations, noise, pressure or other occurrences emitted into the ground, air or water.

- As the causation of environmental damage by a specific installation can often not be proven beyond a reasonable doubt, the UmweltHG establishes a complex system of "presumptions of cause" and exemptions and exclusions from such presumptions. The general presumption of cause is that the damage in question has been caused by a specific installation "if in the circumstances of the particular case an installation is found to have been capable of causing the ensuing damage". The presumption of cause does not apply if the installation has been operated in accordance with permits and conditions imposed on the operator under administrative law. Compliance is presumed if proper control measures were implemented. This means of avoiding strict liability should be an incentive for increased compliance with environmental permits and for additional voluntary control and compliance measures by operators of hazardous installations.
- The owner of the installation is liable in damages if a person is killed or injured or if property is damaged. Liability is limited to 160 million DM. As for "ecological" damage, *i.e.* damage to nature and landscape, the party liable must pay for restoration measures – *e.g.* to restore destroyed biotopes, to recultivate land or to reintroduce endangered species.
- In order to facilitate court action, the act gives the injured party rights to information from the operators of installations and the environmental authorities to enable him to determine whether he has a claim.
- The owners of certain listed installations which are considered to be particularly hazardous are required to have mandatory insurance.

Assessing and Allocating Environmental Liability

In Germany, as in most EC member states, the concept of environmental auditing is still relatively novel. Major European companies and European subsidiaries of US companies have established voluntary internal environmental auditing programmes; in conjunction with transnational mergers and acquisitions of target companies which pose environmental risks, "acquisition audits" are becoming a part of the buyer's due diligence investigation.

Internal environmental compliance audits

To date Germany, like most EC member states, has predominantly relied on the traditional concept of administrative supervision of environmental compliance. Where member states have established mechanisms of environmental self-control by industry, such as the appointment of employees in charge of waste management under German waste legislation, their tasks are sector-specific and do not include the systematic, documented, periodic and objective overall evaluation of environmental performance which character- ises environmental audits. EC Regulation 1836/93, however, has now established an "EC Eco-Management and Audit Scheme" (EMAS) allowing for voluntary participation by companies in the industrial sector, and the International Organization for Standard- ization (ISO) is working on the ISO 14000 series which will set unified standards for environmental management systems.

As an EC regulation, EMAS is directly applicable in the member states. In Germany, the regulation is complemented by the Act on Environmental Audits (*Umweltauditgesetz* (UAG)). The UAG provides for details on the implementation of the regulation. According to the UAG, "accredited environmental verifiers" (*Umweltgutachter*) have to examine the environmental statements prepared by companies participating in EMAS. Verifiers must be independent experts who are examined and accredited by a private organisation.

Acquisition audits

While EMAS provides a regulatory framework for internal com- pliance audits, there are no guidelines for the performance of acquisition audits. Though environmental auditing procedures and techniques show certain parallels to the well-established approaches of financial auditing, essential differences between environmental audits and financial audits concern, *inter alia*, the existence of standards and the accessibility of relevant information. For example, information on environmental compliance and on pollution caused by a given facility is not as readily accessible as financial data required in financial audits. This is, in part, because third parties *e.g.* potential purchasers of an enterprise) do not have a statutory right of access to the files of environmental authorities concerning the target enterprise.

The audit team should thoroughly plan the information-gathering phase of the audit. In practice, the following three steps are generally essential for environmental audits, which are primarily legal exercises:

- collation of information by means of a pre-visit questionnaire, which should already reflect the operational and legal conditions of the target enterprise;
- collation of additional information through structured interviews with the environmental coordinator, management and key employees of the target enterprises as well as interviews with agency officials, if appropriate; and
- physical inspection of the plant, including review of its files as well as soil, soil-air, groundwater and emission sampling.

Major Environmental Initiatives

Environmental legislation will continue to rank among the political priorities in Germany and will thus increasingly determine and influence business operations and strategies. Among the expected legislative projects of the federal government are a Soil Protection Act, an act to expedite and simplify permit procedures, and the project of a unified "Environmental Code".

The federal government has prepared a draft Soil Protection Act, the purpose of which is to prevent harmful changes in the soil through concentrations of environmentally harmful substances and to eliminate risks from contaminated sites. The draft act establishes legally binding definitions of nation-wide standards on soil pollution. If a piece of land is assessed (in accordance with the procedures set out in the draft) and found to be contaminated, the draft provides for differentiated rehabilitation standards, which vary according to the use of the property. The draft authorises the federal government to establish by an ordinance maximum levels, standards for investigation procedures and evaluation criteria for the rehabilitation of contaminated sites, all of which is expected to reduce the costs of investigation and remedial action. The draft act also contains rules on liability for the rehabilitation of contaminated sites. Primarily, the polluter and his legal successors will be liable; but the owner and those entitled to use the property will also be liable. The choice between polluter, owner and other users is made by the competent administrative authority, subject to judicial control by the administrative courts. A provision which allowed those who bear principal liability to seek compensation from others who are liable has been removed from the draft.

The federal government has adopted a draft act to expedite and simplify permit procedures under the Federal Emission Control Act. The draft act aims at adding more flexibility to permit procedures. For instance, the project-bearer may start construction of a new facility prior to the issuance of a permit at his own risk. In case of alterations to existing installations the permit requirement is restricted to major alterations. Another novelty is the integration of clean air legislation and eco-audit legislation. The authority in charge of the permit procedure has to take into consideration, when deciding on permit applications, whether or not the applicant has already prepared documents for an environmental statement.

Finally, one of the most ambitious projects is the planned promulgation of a unified "Environmental Code", a first draft of which has been presented to the public by a group of independent experts. The Environmental Code aims at integrating what is now divided into 20 acts, 61 ordinances and 25 administrative rules. A unified Environmental Code is expected to provide for more effective enforcement, to speed up licensing procedures, and to serve as a model for the harmonisation of European environmental law.

Chapter 8
Environmental Regulation in Hungary

Gabriella Kicska
Baker & McKenzie, Budapest

To meet the requirements of Hungary's developing market economy and the problem of insufficient regulation of the environment, particularly in view of Hungary's wish for convergence with the EC, a new environmental law has been introduced by Act LIII of 1995 on the General Rules of the Protection of the Environment ("the Act"). The Act, which came into effect on 22 January 1996, has replaced the previous legislation (*i.e.* Act II of 1976 on the Protection of the Environment) indicating a progressive legislative process for the protection of the environment.

Sources of Environmental Regulation

The basic structure of laws for the protection of the environment has not been changed: laws passed at the national level prevail, and local regulations must comply with the provisions of such laws. Local authorities (*e.g.* municipalities and regional environmental protection inspectorates) are entitled to pass regulations within their own jurisdictions on certain matters (*e.g.* local regulation of noise and vibration and management of local environmental funds), provided that such regulations do not contravene national laws.

Statutes, Public Laws

The basic legal provisions protecting the environment are contained in: (a) the Constitution (Act XX of 1949 as amended); (b) the Civil Code (Act IV of 1959); (c) the Criminal Code (Act IV of 1978); (d) the Act on Local Authorities (Act LXV of 1990); and (e) the Act.

The Constitution

Section 18 of the Constitution provides that everybody has the right to a healthy environment and the state acknowledges and enforces such rights.

In addition, Section 70/D of the Constitution effective as from 25 June 1990 makes the state responsible for the protection of the natural environment. This amendment was introduced by Act XL of 1990 and reflects a significant change since the collapse of the old regime, under which the protection of the environment was regarded as a theoretical rather than a practical matter.

The Civil Code

Section 345 of the Civil Code makes operators of facilities constituting a danger to the environment liable for damage caused by their operation. Operators may avoid liability only by proving that the damage was unavoidable and unforeseeable. Section 346 of the Civil Code deals with damage caused by more than one operator of such facilities, in which case the operators are jointly and severally liable, unless one of the operators can prove that the damage was caused by the activities of the other.

The Criminal Code

Under Section 280 of the Criminal Code, damage to or destruction of the environment or an object enjoying environmental protection, or any activity resulting in a breach of obligations defined in laws or resolutions of competent authorities which may cause damage to the environment, is a crime punishable by three years' imprisonment. If the damage qualifies as significant or the activity may cause significant destruction to the environment, the crime is punishable by five years' imprisonment. Furthermore, if the damage or destruction is so serious that it is not possible to revert to the status quo, the term of imprisonment may range from two to eight years. Negligent damage to the environment is a misdemeanour punishable by two years' imprisonment, or in case of irreparable damage to the environment by up to three years' imprisonment.

Section 281 of the Criminal Code makes it a crime punishable by three years' imprisonment to unlawfully obtain, export, sell or destroy plants or animals protected as endangered species or under an international treaty, or to unlawfully and significantly change a protected natural area. If wide-spread destruction of plants or animals or irreparable or total destruction of a protected natural area is involved, the punishment is five years' imprisonment.

These provisions of the Criminal Code still apply with different penalties. The increased penalties are effective as from 15 August 1996. Recent amendments to the Criminal Code by Act LII of 1996 increase the penalties for these offences and introduce a new crime addressing the problem of the enforcement of environmental protection regarding hazardous waste. The new Section 281/A provides that unlawful collection, storage, management, deposit or transportation of any waste which may endanger or permanently change human life, health, water, air, land, or which may be dangerous to animals or plants, is a crime punishable by five years' imprisonment. The punishment applies to unlawful deposit of explosive, inflammable or dangerous radioactive materials.

The Act

One of the most important features of the Act is the introduction of a six year National Environmental Programme ("the Programme"). The Programme is to be prepared by the current government and must be evaluated and reviewed by Parliament every two years. The establishment of the Programme guarantees that the overall protection of the environment is dealt with at the highest political and legislative level. Furthermore, it imposes an obligation on the government to report on the implementation of the Programme to Parliament.

The Programme must contain:

(a) a description of the current state of the environment;
(b) environmental goals;
(c) duties necessary for the achievement of the goals and deadlines required for the implementation of the duties; and
(d) tools necessary for the achievement of the goals including planned financial resources.

In practice, point (d) is a sensitive and problematic issue, which may significantly affect the outcome of the current Programme. Pursuant to the official interpretation of the Act, it is not necessary to estimate accurately the funds necessary for the implementation of the current Programme. Since the government is appointed for four years, any government may argue that insufficient funds are available for the implementation or completion of the current Programme. It is likely that the general practice of Parliament will overcome this discrepancy since the government is answerable to Parliament and Parliament approves the funds for the implementation of the Programme.

The Act also provides the opportunity for the public to discuss future regulations in connection with environmental matters, through the National Environmental Council ("the Council"). The Council consists of (a) public organisations registered for conducting activities for the protection of the environment; (b) other professional interest bodies and (c) representatives of Hungarian scientific society appointed by the president of the Hungarian Academy of Sciences. The Council is entitled to submit its opinions to the government before any decision is made on any issues which might have an impact on the environment.

Another characteristic of the Act is that it covers all environmental matters including: overall protection of the natural environment, protection of the land, of the quantity and quality of surface water and groundwater, of the air, of the living environment, of the environment created by human beings (*e.g.* habitation, buildings and other types of plants), protection against dangerous materials and technology, waste, noise and vibration.

Relationship between National, Regional and Local Regulation

The Environmental Protection Inspectorate and the National Public Health Inspectorate have a duty to inspect and evaluate the natural, residential, work and social environment affecting man, including:

- setting air pollution emission standards, control of air pollution and inspection of air quality in enclosed areas;
- setting public health requirements for surface water;
- determination of whether sewage is harmful to public health and inspection of the process of mandatory disinfection of sewage;
- inspection of the toxic effects and delayed harmful effects of waste;
- establishment and enforcement of levels of noise and vibration at work affecting health and the setting and enforcement of levels of noise and vibration harmful to health from mineral extraction, plant operation and dust pollution;
- monitoring compliance with public health duties relating to radioactive materials or equipment emitting radioactivity, electronic and magnetic fields, and inspection of radioactive levels at places of work and their surroundings; and
- inspection of the harmful effects of dangerous materials and the setting and enforcement of appropriate levels.

The above authorities have competence over all persons and entities except for the armed forces. They are under a duty to determine by resolution:

- non-compliance that needs to be corrected and the steps to be taken;
- termination of non-compliance or limitation or suspension of operations if constituting a danger to human health; and
- termination of the use or distribution of materials or objects harmful to health, including if necessary destruction to prevent serious or extensive harm to public health.

The mayor of a municipality and the State Administration Authority have authority over:

- setting plans for the prevention of extraordinary air pollution, including smog warnings;
- limitation, suspension or closure of establishments causing dangerous levels of noise or vibration or requiring such establishments to use another form or method of energy supply;
- where an area is placed under environmental protection, the activity constituting a danger may be prohibited for up to three days, extendable for up to 30 days; and
- compliance with the legal provisions on protection of the environment in local environmentally protected areas and the limitation of traffic in residential areas.

Local authorities can exercise the following powers:

- declaring important local areas and objects as environmentally protected;
- securing the preservation, protection, safe-keeping and restoration of local areas and objects of environmental importance;
- declaring areas as noise protection zones, including zones around an establishment subject to a higher degree of protection;
- establishing local noise and vibration regulations;
- establishing lower air pollution requirements in environmentally protected areas;
- establishing a local plan for the prevention of extraordinary air pollution;
- setting regulations to control air pollution caused by the incineration of leaf litter, garden waste and other activities causing such pollution; and
- organising and operating an environmental protection policy.

Specific Provisions Applicable to Certain Areas of Environmental Regulation

Air Quality

The following laws should be noted:

- Government Decree No. 21/1986 (VI.2) on air pollution and penalties;

- Decree No. 4/1986 (VI.2) issued by the National Office for Environment and Planning on penalties; and
- Departmental Order No. 5/1990 (XII.6) issued by the Ministry of Public Welfare on measuring air pollution.

The operator of a new facility when undertaking construction works or the operator of an existing facility when undertaking expansion or reconstruction must instal and operate technology and adopt procedures in the treatment and processing of materials including waste so as to prevent air pollution. The operators must obtain the approval of the National Public Health Inspectorate on the permissible level of emissions. These are set either by legal provisions or by the particular regional environmental protection authority for its area. Operators of existing establishments must reduce air pollution to the agreed levels, prepare data on such pollution and allow the National Public Health Inspectorate or any other body having duties for the protection of the environment to carry out site inspections.

Operators of existing establishments which cause air pollution must pay an air pollution fine determined by the local National Public Health Inspectorate.

The Minister of Public Welfare determines the list of substances polluting the air and sets air quality limits and the relevant rules on measurement (Departmental Order No. 5/1990 (XII.6.)).

The operators of existing establishments causing air pollution must reduce emissions in the light of expected technological advances. Energy-producing waste may be incinerated in the open air or in traditional installations with the approval of the National Public Health Inspectorate.

Operators must submit data to the National Public Health Inspectorate on the alteration of emission levels within 30 days and substances subject to measurement within one year. Operators must also prepare an annual report on their activities involving air pollution.

The air pollution fine payable by operators increases from year to year (from 20% in the second to 80% in the fifth and subsequent years).

Breaches of air pollution regulations punishable by fine include:

- pollution over permissible limits;

- failure to operate cleaning equipment in accordance with specifications;
- breach of technical specifications; and
- burning waste, stubble, etc. without a licence.

Water Quality

Act LVII of 1995 on Water Courses applies and there are general duties to prevent all adverse effects on the distribution, quantity and quality of water, particularly as it affects the health of consumers and agriculture.

Contamination and pollution of water is prohibited when materials are stored, treated, transported or destroyed, and also in the case of factories, which are obliged as far as possible to treat polluted water so that it may be re-used.

Factories may be built and operated only if sewage water cleaning equipment is installed. In the case of actual or immediate danger of contamination or significant pollution, the water authority may limit or prohibit the activity involved or suspend the operation of the factory if a residential environment or the health of persons may be significantly and directly affected. Factories which contaminate or pollute water or sewage disposal and water purifying plants are subject to fines, compliance with their duties to clean sewage, install or modernise water purifying equipment, criminal prosecution, and liability for contravening other rules and for payment of compensation.

The offence of water pollution may be committed by the discharge of pollutants into surface water, groundwater, reservoirs or water works, by rendering water unusable or by pollution of water caused by construction and operation of a factory without water purifying or sewage storage equipment.

Waste Generation

The following laws should be noted:

- Government Decree No. 56/1981 (XI.18) on control of pro-

120

duction of hazardous waste and activities for their destruction. As from 1 September 1996 this decree has been replaced by Government Decree No. 102/1996 (VII.12).

- Government Decree No. 26/1985 (V.11) on procedures applicable to toxic materials; and
- Government Decree No. 55/1987 (X.30) on importation of substances dangerous to the human environment.

Property owners are under a basic duty to keep their properties clean.

A producer of hazardous waste must keep documents showing the use of materials, and he must notify the Environmental Protection Authority of all hazardous waste produced on a daily and an annual basis. He must also notify the authority of the collection, temporary storage, pre-treatment, use and detoxification arrangements and equipment, including its capacity and the use of such capacity, and he must notify the authority within eight days of any changes.

A producer who does not use or sell his hazardous waste is under a duty to detoxify it.

The Environmental Protection Authority may limit the activity producing hazardous waste or suspend the operation of a facility or equipment involved if the producer is in breach of his obligations and such breach constitutes a direct danger to human health or the surrounding environment. The producer is liable to pay a hazardous waste fine, determined by the authority in the place where the breach occurs, for breach of notification, collection and pre-treatment, transportation, temporary storage or detoxification requirements.

Noise and Vibration

The following laws should be noted:

- Government Decree No. 12/1983 (V.12) on protection from noise and vibration; and
- Departmental Order No. 4/1984 (I.23) on noise and vibration limits.

Facilities and operations emitting noise must be planned, established, expanded or renovated in such a way that their proper operation and any construction work does not cause noise or vibration over permitted limits. These limits are set under a noise limit agreement between the operator and the Environmental Protection Authority, and the operator must ensure that the limits are kept.

All changes which may cause the limits to be exceeded or which may have a significant effect on the limits must be reported to the Environmental Protection Authority within 30 days. The authority should consult the local public health authority and may limit the activities causing the noise or vibration, or in the case of a serious danger to the immediate surroundings may suspend the activities.

In the case of machinery or mechanical fittings, the Minister of Environmental Protection and the other relevant ministers responsible for supervision of their production determine a list of products for which the manufacturer, operator or importer must indicate the noise and vibration characteristics, either on the product itself or in its accompanying documents. If the indicated noise or vibration levels are exceeded, the manufacturer must pay a noise or vibration fine, which may be levied each year and which is determined by the local Environmental Protection Authority of the area where the noise occurs.

Land Protection

There is an obligation to ensure that the quality of land is not damaged by the erection of, alterations to or operations carried on in buildings. The disposal of materials and waste, as well as the establishment of disposal sites must avoid physical, chemical or other pollution of the surrounding land. Any damage caused by breach of this duty must be compensated. In the planning and construction of buildings and other facilities the cost of the work should include the cost of compliance with safety regulations.

Agricultural land may be used for other purposes only with the prior approval of the competent Land Registry, and construction on agricultural land may be undertaken only in exceptional circumstances. If prior approval is not obtained, the land must be restored to its original condition. A land protection contribution or fine must be paid, in addition to any compensation, if the quality of agricultural land is compromised by breach of the Land Protection Regulations or by contamination with dangerous substances. The fine may be levied repeatedly.

Protection of Wildlife

The following laws should be noted:

- Act LV of 1996 on the Protection of Wildlife, Management of Wildlife and Hunting which comes into effect on 1 March 1997;
- Act LIII of 1996 on the Protection for the Natural Environment which comes into effect on 1 January 1997; and
- Act LIV of 1996 on the Protection of Forests which comes into effect on 1 January 1997.

Any activity affecting protected areas (*e.g.* creation of plots of land or construction works) requires the approval or licence of the competent Environmental Protection Authority.

Procedures; Time Periods

Procedures and time periods for environmental permitting are regulated by the provisions of Act IV of 1957 on Public Administration. The procedures must be initiated at the competent ministry or authority and normally take up to 30 days, which may be extended. The resolution of the issuing bodies may be appealed.

Chapter 9
Environmental Regulation in Italy

Pierfrancesco Federici and Angelo Guido Galeotti
Baker & McKenzie, Milan

Sources of Environmental Regulation

Constitutional Provisions

The Italian Constitution of 1948 does not specifically provide rules for environmental protection. It should however be noted that the Italian courts have in many cases over the past two decades interpreted and applied Articles 9 (for the protection of the landscape as well as material objects of historical and artistic importance) and 32 (the right to human health) as being also aimed at protecting the environment.

Statutes

Italian laws on the environment are primarily contained in statutes approved by parliament.

A relatively small portion of such laws were issued before the promulgation of the Constitution, whilst the larger portion directly stem from the EC directives that have been implemented in recent years.

Administrative Regulations and Administrative Interpretations

The Prime Minister and the Minister of the Environment represent the most relevant authorities empowered by statute to issue administrative regulations concerning the environment.

Interpretative documents circulated by administrative authorities do not have the force of law and therefore are not binding. Such documents may however affect the line of reasoning of the courts on the grounds that they embody the opinion of the particular authorities on specific matters.

Relationship between National, Provincial and Local Regulation

The state regions, provinces and municipalities share a certain amount of the jurisdiction over environmental matters. This may give rise to interpretative problems since some statutes are not clear on the scope of the powers and the jurisdiction granted to each authority.

Regions may also promulgate environmental statutes and regulations, in addition to those promulgated by the state. However, certain regions have granted their legislative power to provinces.

It should be stressed that regional and provincial statutes can in no way conflict with laws issued by parliament, although stricter requirements may be set by regulations issued by local authorities.

Enforcement of environmental regulations is mostly by provinces and municipalities and they may take all necessary steps for ensuring compliance. Municipal mayors have wide powers to impose emergency measures in the event that a hazard to the environment requires immediate intervention.

Specific Provisions, Statutes and Regulations Applicable to Certain Areas of Environmental Regulation

Air Quality

Presidential Decree No. 2–3 of 24 May 1988 (DPR 203) is the main regulation in governing matters concerning air pollution.

126

This law, which implements EC Directives 80/884, 84/360 and 85/203 sets out that every plan for building new plants must be notified to the region concerned, which is obliged to ensure that all precautionary steps to prevent pollution are taken and that the maximum level of emission, established by the Prime Minister's Decree of 12 July 1990, is not exceeded. If deemed necessary, the region has the power to lower the maximum level of emission. In all cases both the maximum level of emission and the date operations start must be specified by the authorisations, which set out the requirements and rules according to which the competent authority (normally the province) should monitor plant operations.

The region is given a variety of tools in order to supervise and check the status of air quality. If an authorisation has not been complied with, the region can send warnings, suspend the operation of the plant or, if considered necessary, revoke the authorisation.

The region is also obliged to adopt regional plans in order to improve air quality. In addition to DPR 203 there are other decrees of the Ministry of the Environment which set criteria for formulating plans and gathering air quality data.

Furthermore, specific legislation regulates certain aspects of air quality, such as protection of workers' health, petrol fumes, etc.

Cases of the emission of gas, steam and smoke that may be dangerous to people in public areas have often been considered to be infringements of DPR 203, as well as offences under Article 674 of the Criminal Code.

The decree of the Ministry of the Environment of 12 November 1992 provides general criteria to prevent air pollution of large urban areas as well as guidelines to improve air quality. The decree adopts the provisions of the EC "Green Book on the Urban Environment".

Law No. 549 of 28 December 1993 implements EC Directive No. 92/72 regulating air pollution caused by ozone and addressing issues such as definitions, prevention and control.

Water Quality

Water pollution and any discharges into water and/or soil are governed by Law No. 319 of 10 May 1976 (the "Merli Law").

The law first sets out the authorities in charge of carrying out the various functions in regulating, controlling and supervising the proper use of water and the criteria for discharges: the state (coordination, setting general criteria for the proper use of water, provision of general technical rules, etc.), the regions (formation of general plans for water purification, selling policy for the control of discharges, coordination of the activities of other local authorities); the provinces (registration of all discharges, both public and private, supervision of the application of criteria for the proper use of water) and the local municipalities (control of discharges, issue of authorisation, etc.).

Second, the law provides that every discharge into water and/or soil must be authorised by the relevant authority. The law fixes the maximum pollution levels by reference to their source. If the application for authorisation is not refused within six months from the date of application, the authorisation is deemed to be granted.

Furthermore, the law sets out penalties for violating the water quality provisions: imprisonment (2 months to 2 years) and fines (Lit.50.000 to Lit.10 million).

The Criminal Code and other specific regulations embody other provisions and penalties for particular cases of water pollution, such as contamination or poisoning of water.

Legislative Decree No. 132 of 27 January 1992 implements EC Directive 80/68 on groundwater protection whilst Legislative Decree No. 133 of 27 January 1992 implements EC Directives 76/464, 82/176, 83/513, 84/156, 84/491, 88/347 and 90/415, on the discharge of hazardous substances into water.

Noise

The following EC directives on product noise standards have been implemented by legislative decrees:

- Directives 86/662 and 89/514 were implemented by Legislative

Italy

Decree No. 135 of 27 January 1992 to limit noise from hydraulic or cable digging machines, bulldozers and mechanical shovels.

- Directive 87/405 was implemented by Legislative Decree No. 137 of 27 January 1992 on the permissible sound level for power cranes.
- Directives 88/180 and 88/181 were implemented by Legislative Decree No. 136 of 27 January 1992 to regulate the permissible sound level for lawnmowers.
- Directive 88/594 was implemented by Legislative Decree No. 134 of 27 January 1992 on noise from domestic machines.

Other EC directives on noise pollution which have been implemented are: 79/113, 81/1051, 85/405, 84/533, 84/534, 85/406, 85/407, 85/436, 85/408, 85/409, 84/536 and 85/532.

Law No. 447 of 26 October 1995 provides for general regulation of external and internal noise in order to prevent damage to health. The general guidelines contained in such regulation are specifically directed to the regions in accordance with Article 117 of the Constitution requiring them to implement the regulation by their respective legislative acts. The regulation defines various types of noise causing damage to health and sets the limit of noise allowed in given circumstances. Plans for the control and abatement of noise are also provided under Articles 7 and 8 of the regulation, and Article 10 sets out the penalty, consisting of heavy fines, for infringement of the regulation.

Waste Disposal

Waste disposal is generally governed by Presidential Decree No. 915 of 10 September 1982 (DPR 915), implementing EC Directives 75/442, 76/403 and 78/319, as well as by Law No. 475 of 9 November 1988. The regions may issue statutes and regulations to implement DPR 915.

According to DPR 915 there are three categories of waste: urban, special and toxic and hazardous waste. An annexe to DPR 915 and the ministerial provisions implementing DPR 915 classify every product and substance into one or other category.

Each region has the power to authorise toxic and hazardous waste disposal operations. The authorisation may last for at least five years and governs the following areas: temporary storage, treatment, transportation and final disposal.

Authorisation must be sought for each stage of the waste disposal. Moreover, paragraph 5.3.1. (c) of the ministerial implementation provisions requires the operator to verify that the third party receiving toxic and hazardous waste holds the proper authorisation.

If the terms of an authorisation are not complied with, penalties of imprisonment for up to six months and fines of up to Lit.5.000.000 apply. Furthermore, if non-compliance is repeated or a risk to public health is involved, the authorisation may be suspended or withdrawn.

Law No. 475 requires the person responsible for a waste disposal facility to notify the region each year no later than 28 February of the quantity and quality of waste produced or treated during the previous year. Law No. 475 also provides for a registry or entities authorised to perform waste disposal services.

There are laws specifically regulating particular aspects of waste, such as used oil and "secondary raw materials" (*i.e.* recyclable waste). In particular, the law on secondary raw materials has been the subject of much controversy and has also been modified in a number of respects following the judgment of the Constitutional Court holding the law unconstitutional.

On 6 May 1994 Law Decree No. 279 came into force, making provision for the recycling of waste in general and regulating the storage of hazardous waste in small quantities.

Oil Storage

In accordance with Royal Decree No. 1741 of 2 November 1933, the construction and operation of a mineral oil depot must be authorised by the relevant authority. Non-compliance may involve fines of up to Lit. 400,000 on each member of the board of directors of the enterprise involved and closure of the depot.

Italy

Risk of Serious Accidents

Presidential Decree No. 175 of 17 May 1988 implemented EC Directive 82/501 on the risk of serious accidents in various industrial activities.

The decree obliges enterprises which make use of or store toxic and hazardous substances, listed in the annexes to the decree, to provide the Ministries of Health and the Environment with full details of the activities carried out at the plant and its safety system.

The controlling authorities may close down the plant if they deem it necessary, and there are also criminal sanctions for non-compliance.

Consolidated Health Act

The protection of the environment is also covered by Royal Decree No. 1265 of 27 July 1934 ("Consolidated Health Act"). Article 216 states that an enterprise wishing to embark on an activity involving risk to health as defined by the decrees issued by the Ministry of Health, must notify its intention to do so to the local municipality. For example, a Decree of the Ministry of Health dated 2 March 1987 classifies as enterprises involving a risk to health those enterprises which manage and treat toxic and hazardous waste as defined in DPR 915.

Nevertheless such notification is seldom given in practice. This is because of the extensive and intensive involvement of the local municipality in the setting up of the activity by the enterprise involved and because sanctions for non-compliance are weak.

The Ministry of the Environment

Law No. 349 of 8 July 1986 created the Ministry of the Environment and entrusted it with the task of ensuring the promotion, preservation and regeneration of the environment.

Article 6 requires the government to present to Parliament a plan to implement EC Directive 85/337 in the field of environmental impact assessment (*Valutazione di Impatto Ambientale*

(VIA)). VIA applies to those industrial projects listed in Annexe 1 of the directive. Article 6 also provides that until the implementation of the EC directive the President of the Council of Ministers is in charge of establishing rules for certain categories of projects which may have a significant impact on the environment and which must therefore be submitted to the Ministry of the Environment for approval. These categories are set out in Decree No. 377 of 10 August 1988 (*e.g.* plants for waste disposal, chemical facilities, and oil refineries) and the Decree of 27 December 1988 sets out technical rules by which to evaluate the environmental compliance of the project.

The Ministry of the Environment has been given wide powers in order to operate efficiently and it may even act in the place of local authorities if they fail to carry out provisions of environmental law.

Law 349 has also created a new right of civil action for state and local authorities to claim damages against a person or entity who caused damage to the environment by wilful or negligent conduct in violation of any applicable laws.

A decree of the Ministry of the Environment has recognised a number of organisations whose purpose is the protection of the environment and has given them the right to take part in legal proceedings. These organisations are also entitled to apply to the courts on behalf of persons who have suffered damage as a result of breach of environmental law (Article 91 of the Code of Criminal Procedure).

The Ministry of the Environment also prepares and administers the three-year environmental planning process which sets out the agenda for state intervention in environmental issues, distributes state aid to regions and directs activities in each area. The programme must be approved by the Inter-Ministerial Committee for Economic Planning.

Environmental Permitting Schemes

All applications for state or local authority permits (*e.g.* under DPR 203, the Merli Law, DPR 915) must be made in writing together with the relevant documentation, such as technical plans, emission data and details of the proposed construction.

The applications must be reviewed by a number of authorities, which must prescribe technical requirements for the project.

The procedure is very lengthy, since the timetable is rarely observed. For this reason a recent law has reformed the entire system of administration proceedings in order to introduce stricter obligations on public officials in the performance of their duties.

National Agency for Environmental Protection

Law Decree No. 496 of 4 December 1993 converted into Law No. 61 on 21 January 1994 on "Urgent measures on the re-organization of environment control etc." establishes the National Agency for Environmental Protection (ANPA). The new public entity is under the control of the Ministry of the Environment and is entrusted with various tasks which are especially technical and scientific in nature. Among other matters, ANPA is expected to submit opinions to competent authorities and to cooperate with the European Environment Agency.

Chapter 10
Environmental Regulation in the Republic of Kazakstan

Tamara Barnes
Baker & McKenzie, Almaty

Sources of Environmental Regulation

Article 31 of the Constitution of the Republic of Kazakstan of 6 September 1995 requires the state to set an objective of protecting the environment and its favourable condition for life and health. State officials are to be held accountable for concealing facts and circumstances which may endanger life and health.

Statutes and Regulations

The principal legislation is the Law on the Protection of the Environment of 18 June 1991. This was adopted directly from the Soviet precedent and therefore embodies Soviet environmental policy, the essence of which is in articles 1 and 4. Article 1 provides that the goal of environmental legislation is to prevent economic and other activities from harming the environment. Article 4 provides that a basic principle of environmental protection is the scientifically based blending of economic and ecological interests with ecological interests having priority. To achieve the goal of preventing harm to the environment from economic activity, the Law on the Protection of the Environment creates a system of payments for damage to the environment known as environmental payments. This is a polluter pays system which through a series of regulations attempts to calculate scientifically the cost of the environmental damage caused by an enterprise and internalise that cost to the enterprise. However, a variable in the formulas intended to quantify scientifically the cost of environmental damage includes a delegation of authority to the regional administration which makes calculating and capping environmental payments a political issue rather than a matter of scientific application.

Environmental Payments

The Law on the Protection of the Environment considers the environment a natural resource that may be used as any other resource. Users of the environment are categorised as either general or special users. General users are citizens and other persons who use the environment for daily living free of charge. Special users are those who use the environment for economic or other activities and who must pay for such use. Environmental payments for special use are classified as emissions payments and disposal payments. Emissions payments are generally divided into land, air and water emissions. Disposal payments are generally divided by kind of waste and storage method. The kind of waste is categorised I to IV by harmfulness, category I representing the most harmful waste.

The following table is a typical summary of the annual calculation of environmental payments for an industrial enterprise.

Column 1 lists a representative sample of the types of emissions and disposal payments generally applicable to an industrial enterprise. This list varies depending upon the specific industrial activity of an enterprise. Here the types of payments are representative of mining and electric power production. Items 1. and 2. of this list are for air and water emissions. Item 3. lists the different items for disposal payments.

Column 2 is the quantity of permitted or "normative" emissions and disposal per tonne. Upon application to the Ministry of Ecology an enterprise is issued a permit to emit or dispose of hazardous substances. The quantity of permitted emissions or disposal may be set at either regional or republic level by the Ministry of Ecology, depending upon the quantity and harmful-

Summary of Calculation of Environmental Payments for an Industrial Enterprise

1	2	3	4	5	6	7	8	9	10	11
Name of contaminant, production waste or everyday activity	Permitted discharge (waste, disposal) in tonnes	Actual discharge (waste, disposal) in tonnes	Discharge in excess of the norm	Rate for normative discharge (waste, disposal) in tenge	Amount of payment for normative discharge (waste, disposal) in tenge	Rate for discharge (waste, disposal) in excess of the norm	Amount of payment for discharge in excess of the norm	Total payments in tenge	Payments to the Republic budget	Payments to the Regional budget
1. Pollution of air from harmful chemicals	670,030.120	247,906.160	—	19.50	48,216,170.05	195.00	—	4,834,170.05		
2. Disposal of contaminants with waste water	274.440	82.340	—	5,359.00	441,250.62	53,590.00	—	441,250.62	725,125.51	4,109,044.54
3. Waste disposal:										
– non-toxic industrial waste	167,542.080	696.500	—	16.19	11,276.34	161.90	—	11,276.34	66,187.59	375,063.03
– ashes	718,788.000	299,531.820	—	32.38	9,698,840.23	323.80	—	9,698,840.23	1,691.45	9,584.89
– toxic industrial waste	1,970.100	—	—	32.28	—	322.80	—	—	1,454,826.03	8,244,014.20
– agricultural waste	17,910.000	3,705.380	—	3.30	12,227.75	33.00	—	12,227.75		
– slime in tailing dumps	616,900.000	253,116.060	—	8.36	2,116,050.26	83.60	—	2,116,050.26		

ness of the substance being emitted or disposed of. The quantity of permitted emissions or disposal is established based upon the maximum permissible concentration ("ПДК" or PDK) of the harmful substances contained in the waste. The PDK for each harmful substance is established in a list set by the Ministry of Ecology.

If a plan to increase production raises the concentration of any harmful substance beyond its established PDK, the Ministry of Ecology will only issue a permit for emissions or disposal up to the level of the PDK. This effectively allows the Ministry of Ecology to limit the production of an enterprise.

Column 3 is the actual emissions or disposal by the enterprise.

Column 4 is the amount emitted or disposed of in excess of the normative emissions or disposal.

Column 5 is the per tonne payment rate for emissions and disposal. These rates are set by the head of the regional administration or "*Akim*" based upon the following calculation:

$$\text{Rate per tonne} = \frac{\text{Amount to be spent by the region on its annual environmental programme for the particular emission or disposal}}{\text{Total of the particular emission or disposal in tonnes for all enterprises in the territory}}$$

The regulations provide a series of formulas for calculating the permitted emissions or disposal of particular wastes for each enterprise. However, the amount to be spent by each region on its annual environmental programme is largely within the discretion of the *Akim* of the region. The regional representative body, the "*Maslikhat*", may only approve or reject but not amend the *Akim's* proposed annual budget. Further, these regional representative bodies are generally very weak and not considered instruments for limiting the authority of the regional *Akims*. The only other limit on the *Akim's* authority in this area is found in the Constitution. This provides that the President or the Cabinet of Ministers may alter the decision of a regional *Akim*, although in practice they are reluctant to do so for fear of creating political tension.

Some enterprises have entered into agreements with the *Akims* of their region whereby the *Akim* agrees to maintain environmental payment rates at a certain level. However, these agreements are not legally binding and enforceable. The Republic Civil Code provides that administrative authority over taxation and budgets may not be a subject of an agreement unless otherwise provided for in legislation, and there is no legislative provision allowing the *Akim* to enter into an agreement limiting the *Akim*'s authority to set the annual budget for the regional environmental programme.

The fine for emitting or disposing of quantities of a hazardous substance over the normative quantity is the normative rate multiplied by a specified number (Column 7). The fine is paid only on the quantity emitted or disposed of above the permitted emissions. However, if there is no permit for the particular emission or disposal the enterprise can be fined on the entire volume of the emission. Currently the normative rate is multiplied by 10 to determine the fine for excess emission or disposal. In calculating taxable income an enterprise may not deduct fines for excess emission or disposal as an operating expense.

Columns 10 and 11 contain a breakdown of how much of the total environmental payment is for use at the regional and how much is for use at the republic level. The total environmental payment is made to the Regional Environmental Fund, which then remits 15% of the total to the Republic Environmental Fund. The Regional Environmental Fund is used by the regional department of the Ministry of Ecology with the agreement of the regional administration to finance:

- construction, modernisation, reconstruction and capital repairs of environmental protection facilities of local significance;
- planning, surveying, research and development efforts to develop new types of environmental protection equipment and technologies, automated monitoring systems and technical facilities for this;
- measures to prevent or make up for the harmful social and economic consequences of violations of environmental protection legislation on the region;
- rehabilitation of natural resources affected by economic or other activities;
- public-health protection measures;
- protection and reproduction of flora and fauna;

- establishment of nature preserves, national parks and other natural assets under special protection;
- development of systems of ecological norms; and
- work to evaluate the impact of economic projects on the environment and perform state ecological expert assessments of such projects.

There are no regulations making the regional department of the Ministry of Ecology or the regional administration accountable for the use of the Regional Environmental Fund.

The Republic Environmental Fund is used by the Ministry of Ecology with agreement from the Cabinet of Ministers to finance:

- development and implementation of programmes to fulfil international commitments of Kazakstan;
- research into and development of ecologically safe and resource conservation technologies, standards, norms and rules for environmental protection;
- the creation of ecological data banks;
- international cooperation in environmental protection and the study of foreign experience in environmental management;
- development of facilities for monitoring the environment;
- upgrading of qualifications of environment protection officers, exchanges of experience among them, efforts to increase ecological awareness and ecology-oriented education and upgrading;
- preparation and distribution of reports and information about the state of the environment;
- republic-wide ecological activities; and
- competitions and prizes.

Liability for Past Environmental Damage

The Law on Privatisation provides that a purchaser of an existing enterprise is not liable for environmental damage caused by the enterprise before the purchase. A prospective purchaser is given an opportunity to conduct an environmental audit of an enterprise before purchasing. Upon purchase the purchaser submits an environmental baseline study to the Ministry of Ecology. Once approved by the ministry, the study serves to define the liability of the previous owner for past environmental damage and the liability of the new owner for future environmental damage caused by its operation of the enterprise.

State Regulation

Before commencing operations an enterprise must submit to the Ministry of Ecology an assessment of the impact its operations will have on the environment. The ministry then conducts an expert evaluation of the environmental assessment. If the ministry approves the assessment, the enterprise is given an environmental passport, without which the enterprise may not operate.

After issue of an environmental passport the state continues to monitor an enterprise for compliance with environmental regulations. Generally monitoring is by inspection and on-site methods of monitoring to determine if the enterprise has exceeded the PDK of any particular harmful substance. On-site monitoring consists of testing both at the source of the emission or disposal and also within a surrounding "sanitary zone" where the PDK is set at a lower level. If the PDK is exceeded the enterprise must pay a fine of ten times the normative environmental payment for emission or disposal as described above.

Major Environmental Initiatives

A new draft law on environmental protection has been submitted for approval to Parliament, which has reportedly heavily revised it. The draft when submitted to Parliament contained essentially the current scheme of environmental payments.

Conclusion

The ability of the regional *Akim* to set and change the rate per tonne for environmental payments appears to be largely discretionary, although there are some guidelines for spending of the

Environmental Fund. Environmental payments, in particular the discretion vested in the regional *Akim*, are and remain a significant cause for concern for foreign investors making significant capital investments in Kazakstan. Some companies have sought to insulate themselves against adverse fluctuations in the levels of these payments by entering into formal agreements with the relevant regional *Akim*, although the enforceability of such agreements is uncertain.

Chapter 11
Environmental Regulation in the Netherlands

Hans V. van Ophem
Baker & McKenzie, Amsterdam

Sources of Environmental Regulation

Constitutional Provisions

The Dutch Constitution has since 1983 contained a provision on the role of the government *vis-à-vis* the environment. This provision, Article 21, states that it is the responsibility of the public authorities to care for the habitable nature of the land and to protect and improve the environment. Article 21 was adopted more for political reasons (to stress the importance of a clean environment) than for legal reasons: most environmental laws date from the early 1970s. Article 21 does not grant individuals any rights against the public authorities.

Statutes, Public Laws

The Netherlands has over 20 environmental acts, ranging from the Air Pollution Act to the Soil Protection Act. These are framework acts: as a rule they do not contain specific standards for environmental pollution (*e.g.* noise standards, waste water discharge standards), but they authorise public authorities, especially the government and the Environment Minister, to adopt such standards by general administrative orders and ministerial decrees. Furthermore, the permit authorities derive from the general rules the specific standards they incorporate in a company's environmental permit.

The Environmental Protection Act (EPA) should be particularly noted. The EPA came into effect on 1 March 1993 and is the very core of Dutch environmental law. The EPA brought about many important changes (see also below). One of the major achievements is the replacement of the system of five environmental permits (one for each environmental area, *e.g.* waste, air, noise) by one integrated permit. Furthermore, the EPA sets out a uniform procedure for applying for and granting environmental permits in most of the important environmental areas. The act also contains a uniform system for filing objections and appeals against permits and the specific standards set in the permits. It also contains provisions on environmental impact assessment, public access to documents filed in the application procedures and environmental levies.

General Administrative Orders; Ministerial Decrees

These regulations are issued by the government and the Environment Minister respectively and fill in the details left by the framework acts. Nevertheless, the regulations cover only a relatively small segment of the environmental areas. They may direct the permit authorities to copy the standards set in the regulations into the permits they issue; or they may directly address the relevant industry (*e.g.* import restrictions or the prohibition against discharging waste water into the soil).

Relationship between National, Provincial and Local Regulation

The Netherlands has 12 provinces and approximately 800 municipalities. The provinces and the municipalities are relatively free to adopt their own environmental policies. As a rule, however, if a certain matter is governed by a national law the provinces and municipalities must refrain from regulation in that particular field. In the last few years, more than 20 general administrative orders have been adopted, each one for a different category of usually smaller companies (*e.g.* laundries, garages, LPG gas stations) which in great detail set standards on the effects such companies may have on the environment. The standards relate to noise abatement, prevention of danger, damage and nuisance in general, soil protection measures, etc. Companies in a designated category no longer need an environmental permit. They must, however, observe the standards set in the relevant general administrative order.

Specific Provisions, Statutes and Regulations Applicable to Certain Areas of Environmental Regulation

The Environmental Protection Act

The EPA introduced as from 1 March 1993 a different approach to environmental protection. The following are three important changes (among many changes) brought about by the EPA:

"One-stop-shopping"

Over the years Dutch environmental law burgeoned into a jungle of laws, rules, regulations and permitting systems. Each environmental Act – *e.g.* the Air Pollution Act, the Noise Pollution Act, and the Nuisance Act – had its own permitting system. The EPA introduced the "all-in-one" environmental permit, replacing the existing permits relating to (chemical) waste, nuisance, air and noise pollution with one single permit, the EPA permit. A major exception is the waste water discharge permit (for sewage and surface water) which has to be applied for separately. Existing permits remain valid; they have the same status as (and are regarded to be) a permit issued under the EPA.

"ALARA"

The standards in the EPA permit will be based on the ALARA principle: the company's impact on the environment must be "As

Low As Reasonably Achievable". The EPA designates three stages to reach ALARA:

(a) An EPA permit should lay down those standards which are needed to protect the environment; 100% pollution prevention is the starting point.
(b) If, however, this is not technically feasible (which will, presumably, often be the case), the "best technical means" form the basis for the standards imposed.
(c) If the best technical means are not (financially) feasible, the best practicable means remain the absolute minimum.

"Updating duty"

According to the letter of the law, the updating duty implies that the government will have to tighten permit standards or impose new standards if new technical possibilities provide better environmental protection or if the deteriorating quality of (a part of) the environment so requires. Anyone – including, therefore, environmental groups, local inhabitants and even competitors – may approach the permit authority about this updating duty and, if necessary, demand the tightening of permit standards before an administrative court. Furthermore, the permit authority can require in an environmental permit that the company itself investigates the possibilities of more extensive protection of the environment than is required on the basis of its current permit standards. The results of this investigation then have to be reported to the permit authority.

Air Quality

Before the EPA, the Air Pollution Act had its own permit system, but now the effect on air quality of emissions by companies is regulated in their EPA permits. The Air Pollution Act remains in force. The act and its regulations, of which there are over 20, relate to subjects ranging from type approval of motor vehicles to generally applicable emission standards on nitrogen dioxide.

Water Quality

The most important statutes are the Surface Waters Pollution Act, the Ground Water Act, the Marine Pollution Act and the Act on the Prevention of Pollution by Ships.

The most important act for factories is the Surface Waters Pollution Act. Discharge of waste water into surface water is subject to a discharge permit which contains certain effluent standards. Such permits must be reviewed by the permit authority every four years. The discharge of waste water is subject to levies, the amount of which depends on the volume of the waste water discharged and the degree of pollution caused.

Many of the regulations based on the Surface Waters Pollution Act are the result of implementing EC Directive 76/464 on the discharge of dangerous substances into the aquatic environment. Present regulations require effluent standards for *e.g.* cadmium, mercury, hexachlorocyclohexane (HCH), DDT and pentachlorophenol.

Waste Generation

The Waste Substances Act and the Chemical Waste Act were integrated into the EPA as from 1 January 1994. The new waste legislation mandates the authorities which implement and enforce the EPA to promote qualitative and quantitative waste prevention, recycling and reuse, and to prevent dumping of waste so far as possible. As from 1996, it is prohibited to dump most types of waste. Increasingly, permitting authorities insert waste prevention, minimisation and waste separation standards in EPA permits.

Dangerous waste, which is defined in a separate regulation, may only be disposed of by a licensed processor, and such disposal must be reported to the authorities. Export and import of certain dangerous waste substances are subject to notification requirements.

The environment minister is reluctant to allow exports of waste or hazardous waste, underlining the EC principle of proximity, *i.e.* that waste should be processed as close to its source as possible.

The Courts, however, tend to be very critical of ministerial export bans, in particular on recyclable waste.

Soil Protection and Sanitation

The Soil Protection Act 1994 seeks to encourage industry "voluntarily" to clean up polluted sites and authorises the relevant public authorities to issue sanitation orders to polluters, landowners and long leaseholders. In addition, a regulation for a compulsory indicative soil investigation for some 35,000 companies was adopted.

Clean-up orders

Clean-up orders may be issued by the provinces or the four largest municipalities. They can be issued to the polluter, the owner or the long leaseholder (*"erfpachter"*), regardless of when the pollution occurred. The polluter need not to have acted wrongfully in polluting the soil.

The owner or the long leaseholder may escape a clean-up order if it can prove that:

- during the period in which the pollution occurred, it did not have any substantial legal relationship with the polluter(s);
- it was not directly or indirectly involved in causing the pollution; and
- upon acquiring title (ownership, long lease) to the property it did not know nor could it have known that the property was polluted.

Civil Liability towards the State for Soil Pollution

The liability is fault-based and not retroactive. The Supreme Court had decided that the State of the Netherlands cannot recover its own clean-up costs from companies which polluted the soil before 1975. The Soil Protection Act seeks to overcome this decision. If the state can prove that the polluter knew at the time of pollution prior to 1975 of the serious dangers created by the polluting substances and was grossly negligent by carrying on the polluting acts, then the state may have recourse to the polluter. It is generally believed that only in exceptional cases will the state succeed in recovering clean-up costs for pollution caused before 1975.

Clean-up standards

In 1994 the Netherlands abandoned its A, B and C values (well-known and adopted in many countries) as indications of the degree of pollution and as clean-up standards. Now there are only two values, which are laid down in a ministerial circular but are expected to be enacted soon: the *"Streefwaarde"* or reference value, which indicates that the soil is clean, and the *"Interventiewaarde"* or intervention value, which indicates that the soil is seriously polluted and requires cleaning up.

The extent of clean-up generally depends in practice on a cost comparison between the so-called "multifunctional" clean-up (a fully-fledged clean-up of all contaminants to their respective reference values so that virtually no pollution is left in the soil) and the so-called "isolation" clean-up (the pollution is contained at the site and constantly or regularly monitored, sometimes combined with removal of some "hot spots"). If there is an "extreme cost difference" (a mathematical formula exists to establish this) between a multifunctional and an isolation scenario, the latter may be chosen. A clean-up plan requires approval by the province or one of the four largest municipalities.

Environmental Permitting Schemes

Procedures; Time Periods

In general an application for an environmental permit must contain data on the applicant, the facility, *e.g.* its size, a description of its production process, storage facilities, energy consumption, a description of the anticipated pollution and pollution prevention or reduction measures.

An application fee is payable, the amount of which will largely depend on the nature of the facility and sometimes the amount of machine power being installed.

The following scheme applies to most of the common environmental permits.

The application for a permit is sent to the permit authority (usually the municipality or province in which the facility is located). The permit authority sends the application to the labour inspectors and environment inspectors for comment (copies of which will be sent to the applicant). The permit authority may ask the applicant for additional data.

As soon as possible but in any case within three months, the permit authority must issue a draft permit and transmit it to the applicant and the labour and environment inspectors. In case of very complicated or controversial applications, *e.g.* a large chemical plant, this time period may be extended.

Within two weeks of transmission, the draft permit or a summary of it must be published in a newspaper and must be deposited for public inspection at the municipal hall. The applicant may request that certain data (company secrets) be kept confidential and not deposited.

Within one month of deposit of the draft permit, anyone can file objections in writing with the permit authority. Copies of objections filed will be sent to the applicant. The labour and environment inspectors can also file their opinions within one month of deposit.

Anyone may ask the permit authority to convene a hearing on the draft permit, which hearing must also take place within one month of deposit of the draft permit.

As soon as possible but in any case within six months of the date of application, the permit authority must rule definitively on the application (*i.e.* reject it or issue a permit). In the case of very complicated or controversial applications the permitting authority may extend this six month deadline.

Within two weeks the permit authority must publish and deposit its decision (*e.g.* the permit) for public inspection. Within six weeks of deposit appeals can be filed with the administrative court of the State Council in The Hague by the applicant or those who have filed objections against the draft permit. After this six week period the permit enters into force, unless the chairman of the administrative court has decided – upon application made to the court – that the permit or part of it should not enter into force until the court has definitively decided on the appeals that may have been filed.

It is a feature of this scheme that the permit authority is under an obligation to decide on the application and the issue of the permit as soon as possible. The periods allowed are all maximum periods. The time schedule, therefore, depends largely on the speed of the permit authority and whether objections are filed.

Entities

- The Environment Minister: certain permits/approvals under waste legislation.
- The provinces: permits under the Surface Waters Pollution Act (also Water Boards), EPA permits for, as a rule, the larger companies.
- The municipalities: EPA permits for most companies.

Some of the permits may be issued by other entities, depending for instance on the location of the factory or the surface water involved.

Enforcement of Environmental Regulation

Administrative Enforcement

The public authorities responsible for implementing the relevant regulations are responsible for administrative enforcement. The administrative sanctions for violation of permit standards include an order for close down and a notification that a violation must be remedied, failing which the government will do so, at the company's cost. This instrument was used by the government frequently until the introduction of the *"dwangsom"*, a penalty imposed as a sum to be paid over a period of time or upon each offence in order to entice the offender to remedy the offence concerned.

The *dwangsom* is now the most frequently used tool of administrative enforcement. Although there is no maximum for the amount set, it must be in reasonable proportion to the damage done and the intended effect, *i.e.* remedy by the offender. The offender must be given the opportunity to rectify the violation before the penalty is imposed.

Criminal Enforcement

Criminal enforcement is the responsibility of the public prosecutor. Companies, usually a legal entity of the BV type, can be criminally prosecuted and convicted, but condemned only to pecuniary penalties (up to NLG 1 million). Corporate officers (*"bestuurders"*) and directors (*"commissarissen"*) can also be criminally liable. If an officer had knowledge of the criminal act being committed, was authorised to prevent such act but nevertheless wilfully accepted that the act was committed, the officer can be held criminally liable. Punishment ranges from fines to imprisonment. Only few officers, and even fewer directors, have been criminally prosecuted and convicted. The relevant authorities, however, seem to be less hesitant than in the past to prosecute officers personally.

In practice, the public prosecutor often makes an offer to a company that it pays a certain amount to the state in order to prevent further prosecution. The amount will depend on *inter alia* the nature and environmental effects of the violation involved.

Civil Enforcement

If a company's business (plant) causes damage or a nuisance (noise, vibrations, odour, air pollution) and can be said to have done so wrongfully, the injured party may seek a court order to have the company cease its damaging activities, even if such activities are covered by a permit. A permit does not indemnify against

152

wrongful acts. In practice, this civil route is not often taken because of the high costs involved. Usually, private individuals ask their local government to take enforcement measures (as described under Administrative enforcement).

As a rule, environmental pressure groups have legal standing and can ask for injunctions against activities damaging the particular environmental interest of their group.

Civil liability for environmental damage is based on wrongful acts. There are some exceptions: as from 1 February 1995 the Civil Code imposes strict liability on the person who in the course of his business uses or possesses dangerous substances (as defined) at the time when the damage occurred. This applies in particular to persons storing or transporting dangerous substances. The act does not have retroactive effect. Certain limitations on the amount of damages to be paid may apply to certain categories of persons found liable.

Major Environmental Initiatives

Internal Environmental Care System

When issuing environmental permits, the government as a rule urges the largest 10,000 companies to establish an environmental care system. The environmental care system is anticipated to be proportionate to the size of the company involved: only the largest companies will be required to have a system, which may be compared with the EC Eco-management and Audit Scheme (EMAS). Industry is already in the process of developing a standard environmental care system in cooperation with the government. Some 300 of the largest companies are expected to be required by law to issue annual environmental reports in the near future.

Packaging Materials Covenant

In 1991 the Environmental Minister and the Dutch industry-based Foundation for Packaging and the Environment signed a covenant aiming to reduce waste from packaging and promoting recyclable packaging. Only those companies represented in the Foundation are bound by the covenant. One of the commitments of the companies represented by the Foundation is further to limit the use of PVC in packaging by alternatives which are less harmful to the environment. It is unclear what will happen with this covenant after the adoption of the Packaging and Packaging Waste Decree (described below).

Draft Packaging and Packaging Waste Decree

The Environment Ministry recently published a draft regulation on packaging and packaging waste designed to implement the EC directive of 20 December 1994. The regulation is intended to take effect in the second half of 1996.

According to the draft regulation producers or importers (as defined) of products must ensure that the following recovery/recycling goals be reached:

- 65 % by weight of the packaging waste must be recovered;
- 45 % by weight of the packaging materials contained in packaging waste must be recycled;
- 15 % by weight for each packaging material.

These recovering/recycling goals stated in the draft regulation are the highest goals allowed by the EC directive.

Producers/importers must put in place a take-back and recovery/recycling scheme in order to reach the goals. Producers/importers are not required to arranged for collection of household packaging waste door-to-door, rather from a central municipal collection point. The municipalities remain responsible for door-to-door collection of household waste, including packaging waste.

Producers/importers are required, however, to ensure separate packaging waste collection at companies, but the costs involved are for the account of the companies disposing of their packaging waste.

Producers/importers are also required to "take measures" for quantitative and qualitative minimisation of packaging. This requirement is not specified further: this is because the EC directive does not contain specific prevention requirements.

A burdensome requirement in the draft regulation is a yearly reporting requirement (to the Environment Ministry) on the producer/importer showing how he executed his recovery and recycling requirements under the regulation, what the results were and what measures he took to enhance quantitative and qualitative minimisation.

If, however, a producer/importer is meeting his requirements under the regulation through a joint scheme set up by his industry branch, he may refer to the report to be submitted by his branch. The draft regulation assumes that most companies will join their branch organisation's efforts to set up take-back and recovery/recycling schemes, which branch in its turn will wish to make covenants with other relevant industries.

The draft regulation has copied from the EC directive the requirements on concentration levels of heavy metals present in packaging (see Article 11 of the EC directive on the concentration levels of lead, cadmium, mercury and hexavalent chromium present in packaging or packaging components).

Waste Disposal Contributions Act

Under the Waste Disposal Contributions Act 1994 those who import or market a product in the Netherlands may decide to agree on a waste disposal contribution to be paid per product to the government. The reason for this may be to prevent stricter legislation. The contributions will be used for the collection and disposal of the waste from the products.

The agreement is voluntary, and some businesses in a particular sector of importation or marketing may refuse to join. If, however, a significant majority of businesses in the sector do enter into the agreement, they can ask the Environment Minister to declare their agreement binding on all businesses in the sector, even those who had refused to join the agreement. A waste disposal contribution on cars has been declared generally binding on all businesses in the sector.

It has been argued that the act violates Article 30 of the EC Treaty, as its aim is said to be the protection of industry from unfair competition rather than environmental protection. However, the act has not yet been challenged in court.

Products and the Environment

The Environment Minister recently issued a memorandum on products and the environment in which she stressed the need for increasing attention from the business community for developing environmentally friendly products. She introduced the concept of a company internal environmental care system particularly focused on products.

The Environment Minister is in effect asking companies to expand their environmental care systems with a chapter on product development. The EC EMAS regulation already contains a requirement relating to product development: one of the principles of a company's environmental policy is that the environmental impact of all new products be assessed in advance.

Product-related environmental law is clearly developing. Depending on the efforts of the business community towards developing environmentally friendly products and the results of these efforts, the Minister's memorandum may prove to be the start of a trend towards a more direct regulation of products.

Chapter 12
Environmental Regulation in Poland

Jur Grusczyński and Waleria Skarżyńska
Baker & McKenzie, Warsaw

Sources of Environmental Regulation

Constitutional Provisions

The Constitution is the highest act setting norms which other regulations may not violate. The Constitution includes only two provisions which refer to the natural environment. According to these provisions the Republic of Poland protects and warrants the reasonable maintenance of the natural environment. All citizens have the right to enjoy the natural environment and are obliged to preserve it.

Statutes, Public Laws

Statutes (laws) are passed by parliament. The procedure is in three stages: first, adoption of the statute by the *Sejm* (the lower chamber) by a simple majority of at least half the members; second, amendments by the *Senat* (the higher chamber), which are binding unless the *Sejm* rejects them by an absolute majority; third, signature by the President, who may, however refuse to sign and may return the statute to the *Sejm* for reconsideration; if the *Sejm* adopts it again by a majority of two-thirds the President is obliged to sign.

Regulations or Administrative Interpretations

The Council of Ministers, the Minister for the Protection of the Environment, Natural Resources and Forestry ("Minister for the Environment") and other ministers are authorised to issue implementing regulations which stipulate environmental standards. Rural and municipal communes (the smallest division in local government, called "*gmina*") and *voivodes* (local organs of general governmental administration) are authorised to adopt local regulations.

Relationship between National, Provincial and Local Regulation

Voivodes may establish temporary limitations or bans on emissions, define specific forms of nature preservation and issue other environmental bans and orders. Commune councils are entitled to establish some form of nature preservation and adopt bans and orders which may limit the time of operation or the use of technical equipment and/or transport or to adopt local development plans. Such plans may specify the conditions for and the manner of development and exploitation of land. The most important rules for environmental protection are in statutes and the relevant implementing regulations issued by the Council of Ministers, the Minister for the Environment and other ministers. These rules are binding nationally. Local regulations apply to detailed issues and are reserved for immediate protection of the environment. However, all regulations must comply with the constitutional rules and in case of local regulations must not exceed the limits of the statutory authorisation under which they are issued.

Specific Provisions, Statutes, and Regulations Applicable to Certain Areas of Environmental Regulation

Air Quality

Under the law on environmental protection a permit for the maximum emission allowed will be issued for each investment project. These permits seek to prevent excess over admissible concentrations of pollutants in the air and in the long term to reduce or eliminate certain other pollutants. The permit specifies the types and volumes of pollutants which may be emitted and gives detailed terms on which the emission may be made. It may also define obligations to protect the environment against air pollution.

Additional regulations define the permitted concentrations of certain air pollutants which vary according to their location, permitted concentrations of cadmium, lead and dust and permitted volumes of sulphur dioxide, nitrogen dioxide and dust emitted by combustion processes.

Water Quality

Water may be used under the following rights to its use:

- Common: the right granted by law to each person and relating to surface waters owned by the state; this right is the right to satisfy personal needs and the needs of a household or a farm (without using special equipment) as well as for recreation, tourism, water sports and fishing.
- Ordinary: the right of the owner of land to exploit his own water and underground water to satisfy his own needs and the needs of his household or farm, excluding exploitation of water for industrial purposes or for spray irrigation; and
- Special: any other rights; any special exploitation of water requires an effluent permit which regulates the use of water.

An economic entity is obliged to obtain a water permit authorising use of surface and underground water, disposal of sewage into a watercourse or the soil, storage of sewage and other waste material particularly close to rivers and supply of water by means of installations running through the land of third parties.

A permit is not required for the disposal of sewage into the public sewage system. Such disposal is made on the basis of an agreement with the commune water and sewerage companies.

Waste Generation

Under the Law on Environmental Protection waste materials are defined as products not useful in the place and at the time of their production and hazardous to the environment. Economic entities are obliged to protect the environment against pollution or destruction by or other adverse effects of waste materials.

The import of waste materials from abroad is allowed only under an individual permit granted by the Chief Inspector of Environmental Protection. The permit may be issued only for waste materials designated for re-use which are not available in Poland and on the condition that wastes will not cause an increased threat to the environment and will not increase the total amount of waste materials stored in Poland. The import of dangerous waste from abroad is banned.

Especially hazardous waste materials comprise materials and substances listed in the Decree of the Minister for the Environment dated 3 August 1993. For such waste, the economic entity that produces them must obtain a decision for their elimination or neutralisation. A permit obtained from *voivodes* or commune authorities is required for the storage of any waste products. Such permit may be amended at any time.

The Decree of the Council of Ministers dated 30 September 1980 on protecting the environment against waste materials and other contamination, the Atomic Law dated 10 April 1986 and the Law on Poisonous Substances dated 21 May 1963 deal with the elimination and neutralisation of waste and the production and use of waste material which may contaminate, cause infection or contain radioactive elements. According to the Atomic Law production, processing, storage, transport or use of radioactive materials and radioactive waste products and the construction and exploitation of storage installations requires a permit from the President of the State Atomic Agency.

Noise

The Law on Environmental Protection and implementing regulations such as the Decree of the Council of Ministers dated 30

September 1980 on protecting the environment against noise and vibrations require the local council to issue individual noise decisions in all cases when noise levels from industrial activities are exceeded in public areas.

Environmental Permitting Schemes

Procedures

Any decision taken in connection with the implementation of regulations on environmental protection is an administrative decision. This means that it can be subject to review by a higher tier authority and subsequently it can be subject to appeal to the Supreme Administrative Court on points of law. Environmental regulation is also carried out under the procedures for town and country planning. Each new investment project requires an environmental impact assessment and the approval of the environmental authorities before a construction permit is granted. The scope of the environmental impact assessment and the type of approval depends on the type of investment project concerned.

Entities

The Minister for the Environment has a secondary policing function, sets environmental quality standards in the form of secondary legislation and reviews appeals from the decisions of *voivodes*.

The *voivoda* is the governor of one of the 49 provinces. *Voivodes* set individual emission standards on the basis of regulations issued by the minister and grant all necessary environmental permits, *i.e.*, air emission permits, water discharge permits, waste disposal permits for the establishment of protective zones, etc. They are primarily responsible for the scheme of environmental permitting.

The State Inspectorate for Environmental Protection is an enforcement agency. It is directly subordinate to the Minister for the Environment and is therefore not subordinate to the *voivodes*. The inspectors have the right of entry onto industrial premises, can impose fines or suspend the activity being carried out.

Local authorities are the municipal and rural communes that were set up as distinct from the state public entities and were elected in 1990 for the first time since 1950. They took over responsibility for all matters not restricted to governmental authorities and are responsible for land use planning and the provision of public utility services (mainly water supply, domestic sewage discharge and the management of household waste).

Time Periods

The time periods for resolving matters in administrative proceedings are set out in the regulations on administrative procedure:

- immediately – in case of issues which may be considered on the basis of documents presented by a party together with the proper application or on the basis of facts and evidence publicly known or officially known by the administrative body;
- within one month – in case of issues which require the conduct of preliminary proceedings such as completion of documents and other evidence;
- within two months – in case of especially complicated issues; and
- within one month – in case of appeal proceedings.

These time periods do not include periods provided by the laws for performance of certain activities, periods of delay caused by a party or reasons beyond the control of the administrative body involved.

Appeals against decisions taken at first instance should be made to the supervisory body within 14 days. In the case of binding decisions there is a right of appeal to the Supreme Administrative Court.

Enforcement of Environmental Regulation

Administrative Liability

Enforcement is by *voivodes*, inspectors of the State Inspectorate of Environmental Protection and commune authorities. Sanctions are:

- revocation of permits (by *voivodes*);
- suspension of infringing activities (by inspectors of the State Inspectorate of Environmental Protection);
- suspension of the operation of machinery (by *voivodes*);
- imposing reinstatement regulations (by *voivodes*); and
- imposing obligations on economic entities to protect water against contamination (by commune authorities).

Fines

Fines may be imposed by inspectors of the State Inspectorate of Environmental Protection and in some cases by commune authorities for the infringement of regulations or stipulations of administrative decisions. There is no need to show fault. The imposition of a fine does not affect liability for damages under the civil law, nor does it protect the person responsible from criminal liability.

Fines may be imposed for:

- disposal of waste without a permit or in contravention of the terms of a permit;
- air pollution in contravention of the terms of relevant decisions;
- storage of waste in contravention of the terms of storage; and
- exceeding acceptable levels of underground water extraction.

Civil Liability

Under the Civil Code economic entities are liable for damage caused by acts or omissions having a noxious effect on the environment. Liability is strict.

The injured party needs to prove only that he has suffered damage caused by the operation of the enterprise. Operating in accordance with the relevant environmental regulations is no defence; the only defences are *force majeure* or the fault of the injured person or of a third party who was exclusively responsible for the damage. *Force majeure* means an event which has a character external to the operations of the enterprise, which was unexpected and could not be prevented. Third parties do not include employees, subordinates to an enterprise, its organs or its subcontractors.

Criminal Liability

Breach of regulations for environmental protection may result in criminal liability.

The most typical sanctions are:

- imprisonment for a period from three months to three years;
- a fine between 250,000 and 500,000,000 zlotys (approximately US$25 to 12,500); and
- public works without remuneration for between 20 and 50 hours per month from three months to three years.

Individuals responsible for a crime are subject to criminal liability. This also applies to managers or chiefs of the section of an enterprise responsible for environmental protection and water economics. There is no criminal liability on legal entities nor automatic liability on the board of management of an economic entity unless they can be proved to have been at fault.

Economic Indicators

The incentives for environmentally friendly economic activity are at present limited, although there is exemption from income tax for taxpayers – other than for state enterprises, cooperatives, and business entities – whose statutory objectives constitute activity in the fields of environmental protection.

Major Environmental Initiatives and Pending Proposals

The fact that the Water Bill and Waste Bill have been subject to continuous debate between the government and industry for about four years shows how deeply the legislation is expected to influence the conditions of doing business in Poland. The bills are still before parliament.

These new laws are expected to impose the following:

- the obligation to draw up a legally binding waste balance sheet;
- fees for the storage of waste as distinct from fees for depositing waste;
- fines for improper storage of waste – up to 5% of the annual fee for one day;
- the obligation to calculate (on the same principles as taxes) the fees for the use of the environment payable to the National Fund of Environmental Protection and Water Management and communes; and
- a two-year period of adjustment after which new permits would be granted.

Chapter 13
Environmental Regulation in the Russian Federation

Jean A. Brough*
Baker & McKenzie, Moscow

Sources of Environmental Regulation

Constitutional Law

The Constitution of the Russian Federation of 12 December 1993 includes several articles on environmental protection. Article 38 provides that land owners may not act to the detriment of the environment while exercising rights to their land. Article 42 states that citizens shall have the right to a safe environment, to reliable information about the state of the environment and to receive restitution for damage to their health and property resulting from acts harmful to the environment. Article 58 stipulates that citizens are obliged to preserve nature and the environment and use due care when extracting natural resources.

Civil Code

The Civil Code includes several articles on the protection of the environment. Article 1 states that restrictions on the movement of goods and services will be imposed in order to adequately protect the environment. Article 209 provides that the possession, use and disposal of land and of other natural resources will be restricted if such actions adversely affect the natural environment.

*The author gratefully acknowledges the assistance of Jonathan Wise (summer associate, Baker & McKenzie, Moscow) in the preparation of this chapter.

Statutes and public laws

Federal Law No. 2060–1 of 19 December 1991 on the Protection of the Natural Environment ("EPL") is the primary and most comprehensive legislation on environmental protection. The aim of the legislation is threefold:

- to regulate the interaction of society and the environment in order to preserve and protect man and the environment from the harmful effects of industry;
- to restore and protect the environment; and
- to prosecute actively individuals and organisations who violate environmental laws.

Other primary pieces of legislation on environmental protection include Federal Law No. 174-FZ of 23 November 1995 on Environmental Expert Appraisals (the "Appraisal Law"), and the Regulations for the Licensing of Certain Kinds of Activities in the Sphere of Environmental Protection, as approved by Decision No. 168 of the Federal Government of 26 February 1996 (the "Licensing Regulations").

Regulations or Administrative Interpretations

The executive authority for an area (equivalent to the local government authority) may enter into a contract with an enterprise which defines and regulates the use of natural resources in that area and specifically sets out:

- the rights and obligations of the enterprise using the resources;
- the payment required for the use of natural resources and for the right to exploit the environment by way of emitting pollutants;
- the liability of parties for non-compliance with the contract;
- compensation payable for harm caused to the environment; and
- the procedure for resolving disputes.

A licence is issued to the enterprise by the appropriate government body, which also establishes the limits of permitted emissions. In

Moscow these functions are performed by the Norm-setting and Licensing Division of the Moscow Environmental Protection Agency or *Mosgorpriroda*.

Relationship between National, Provincial and Local Regulation

The implementation of legislative policies is divided between the Federal Assembly of the Russian Federation, the Government of the Russian Federation (including especially empowered state authorities), the Republics of the Russian Federation, specific regional authorities, and local self-administration authorities. The legislation (Articles 6–10 of the EPL) provides a comprehensive list of the powers granted to each of these bodies.

Specific Provisions, Statutes and Regulations Applicable to Certain Areas of Environmental Regulation

Air, Water and Soil Quality

Article 26 of the EPL stipulates that the quantity of dangerous pollutants and harmful biological substances emitted into the air, water and soil be fixed to protect the interests of the environment and human health. When setting the limit account is taken of the production capacity of the facility involved and the known dangers of the relevant substance (Article 27).

Waste disposal

The disposal of waste, including the authorisation of landfill sites, is regulated by local government authorities. Article 54 of the EPL prohibits the deposit of waste into public waterways or underground aquifers.

In accordance with Article 1 of the Licensing Regulations, the utilisation, storage, shipment, placement, dumping and disposal of industrial and other waste materials requires a licence from the Federal Government. Licences are also required to undertake activities which involve the conduct of environmental audits and activities involving the conservation of nature. These licences are issued by the Ministry of Environmental Control and Natural Resources Protection and its various branches ("the Ministry"). The Licensing Regulations detail the types of documents to be submitted with an application for a licence. The decision to grant or reject an application must be made by the Ministry within 30 days of reviewing the application. In certain cases the decision can be extended by an additional 30 days. Licences are issued for three years and are not transferable.

Noise, Vibrations, Magnetic Fields and other Harmful Physical Effects

Enterprises, institutions, organisations and individuals must take all necessary steps to prevent intensive industrial noise and/or vibrations which would be harmful to either the environment or persons (Article 53 of the EPL).

The government sets maximum levels of acceptable industrial noise and any infringement of these limits may result in the suspension or termination of the activity. The maximum permissible levels of noise, vibration, magnetic fields and other harmful physical effects are regulated in the same way as emissions into the air, water and soil.

The Ozone Layer

Article 56 of the EPL regulates the production and use of chemical substances that destroy the ozone layer. Article 56 provides that enterprises, institutions and organisations are obliged to reduce and subsequently cease to produce and use chemical substances which are harmful to the ozone layer. A list of harmful chemical substances and production waste have been approved by state bodies of the Russian Federation specially authorised in the field of environmental protection.

Radioactive Substances

Article 29 of the EPL provides that the level of radioactive substances in the environment and food products will be fixed in magnitudes that do not endanger human health and genetic stock. These levels will be approved by specially authorised state bodies in the field of environmental protection, sanitary and epidemiological supervision.

Article 50 of the EPL provides that enterprises, institutions, organisations and individuals are obliged to observe rules for the production, storage, transportation, use, removal and dumping of radioactive substances. Those who fail to observe the rules for handling radioactive materials will lose the right or be temporarily deprived of the right to use such materials.

Agriculture

Enterprises, organisations and individuals in the agricultural sector must adopt measures to protect the environment from the harmful effects of their activities (Article 46 of the EPL). They must also follow guidelines established by the Committee for Public Health and Epidemiological Supervision regulating the use of chemical substances in agriculture (Article 51 of the EPL). Use of a chemical not on an approved list compiled by the Ministry of Agriculture as permissible must be approved by the Committee for Public Health and Epidemiological Supervision.

The amount of mineral fertilizers, plant protection substances, growth stimulants and other chemicals which may be used is based upon a dose which is harmless to human health. These amounts are regulated in the same way as emissions into the air, water and soil (Article 30 of the EPL).

Environmental Permitting Schemes

Commissioning of Facilities

A facility will only be commissioned if it meets all the environmental requirements stipulated by its licence issued by the state (Article 44 of the EPL). Facilities will not be commissioned if they lack modern technologies, installations and equipment to purify and neutralise waste, control emissions and monitor pollution of the environment.

Regulations for the Operation of Enterprises

Emissions or deposits of noxious substances are allowed on the basis of a permit issued by the state authorities of the Russian Federation. This permit sets out the regulations governing the maximum level of permissible emissions (Article 45 of the EPL). Where an enterprise is in the process of upgrading its facilities to comply with these maximum limits, temporary limits may be established until pollution control mechanisms are in place.

If the regulations are breached, the operation of the enterprise will be suspended or terminated, and in certain cases the financiers of the enterprise may be instructed to suspend their funding.

Environmental Insurance and State Environmental Appraisal

Environmental Insurance

Voluntary and mandatory insurance exists for enterprises, institutions, organisations and individuals and covers their property and income in the event of environmental or natural disasters, accidents or catastrophes (Article 23 of the EPL).

State Environmental Appraisal

State environmental appraisals are undertaken to ensure that economic and other activities meet present environmental safety expectations and standards. State environmental appraisals are mandatory regardless of the cost or ownership of the particular enterprise or project (*i.e.* including foreign-owned enterprises) and must precede the adoption of economic decisions the execution of which may be detrimental to the environment (Articles 35–39 of the EPL). The managers of enterprises, institutions and organizations, other officials and staff workers and even private persons will bear responsibility should the enterprise fail to comply with the conclusions of an appraisal.

The general provisions of the EPL are supplemented by the specific criteria of the Appraisal Law. The Appraisal Law sets out in detail the manner in which such appraisals are conducted, the persons who are authorised to act as appraisal experts and the types of investigations which an appraiser can conduct. It also provides a list of rights for companies undergoing an appraisal to ensure that the appraisal is conducted in accordance with legislative procedures. The law also stipulates the mechanism for appeal from the findings of the appraiser. Individuals violating the provisions of the Appraisal Law may face criminal, civil or administrative liability.

Enforcement of Environmental Regulation

Environmental Monitoring

The environmental monitoring system consists of the State Environment Monitoring Service and the State Environment Monitoring System. Officials in the State Environment Monitoring Service observe overall changes in the environment and make this information available to interested parties. The State Environment Monitoring System makes and enforces policies on the environment. Article 70 of the EPL states that the State Environment Monitoring Service has the right to:

- visit enterprises, irrespective of their form of ownership, and to review any documents they believe necessary for the performance of their professional obligations;

- check the purification installation and other neutralising equipment and monitoring equipment of facilities;
- issue permits regulating emissions and deposits of noxious substances;
- establish limits on emissions;
- require an environmental appraisal;
- require correction of any problem identified;
- initiate administrative or criminal prosecutions against any person infringing the regulations and enforce compensatory awards against such persons; and
- make decisions on the restriction or suspension of the activities of the enterprise.

Penalties

Certain infringements are subject to a fine (Article 84 of the EPL). In the case of citizens the fine will be 1–10 times the minimum monthly wage; in the case of officials the fine will be 3–20 times the minimum monthly wage. Notwithstanding the amounts specified in the EPL the fines for industrial pollution and waste disposal have been adjusted (although the amounts are not precisely defined) by later legislation, including the "Procedure of Defining and Readjusting Payments for Polluting the Environment, Disposing of Wastes and other Types of Harmful Acts", confirmed by the Russian Government in Resolution No. 632 of August 18, 1992. Infringements subject to a fine are:

- non-observance of standards, regulations or other rules protecting the environment;
- non-performance of obligations to carry out an environmental appraisal, or non-performance of requirements contained in the findings of an environmental appraisal;
- infringement of planning, construction or operational requirements;
- polluting the environment or causing harm to human health or the environment;

- failure to comply with orders from authorities carrying out environmental monitoring;
- exceeding established permissible levels of noise, vibrations, magnetic fields or other harmful physical actions;
- damage to or destruction of the environment;
- non-performance of clean-up requirements;
- violation of requirements relating to waste; and
- production and use of prescribed chemical substances and/or industrial waste having a harmful effect on the ozone layer.

The payment of fines does not exempt the individual or organisation from civil liability (Article 84 of the EPL).

Civil Liability

Section XIV of the EPL requires enterprises, institutions, organisations and individuals polluting the environment to make full compensation for damage caused to the environment by their actions (Article 86). Compensation is based either on the amount of the damage caused or on the actual cost of reparation. If there are several found liable, the damages are shared in proportion to the liability of each. With the consent of the proper authority an entity found liable may carry out clean-up at its own cost.

Harm caused to the health of an individual as a result of the activities of enterprises must be compensated in full. When calculating the extent of the harm caused, the following criteria are taken into account (Article 89 of the EPL):

- the degree of loss of fitness for work suffered;
- the cost of treatment, care and other expenses including lost professional opportunities;
- the cost arising from the need to move and change his way of life;
- trauma; and
- the inability to have children or the increased risk of bearing children.

Enterprises and individuals have the right to bring lawsuits in the courts or to commence arbitration.

Other Matters affecting the Environment

Obligations on Foreigners

All foreign legal and physical persons operating in the Russian Federation must observe the requirements of the EPL and bear any liability arising from any infringement of it (Article 3 of the EPL).

Economic Incentives

The government has adopted incentives for organisations and enterprises which take steps to protect the environment (Article 24 of the EPL). These incentives include:

- tax and other concessions to enterprises which adopt low-waste or no-waste technologies in their production processes, use secondary resources or undertake any other programmes or activities with an environmentally beneficial effect;
- government funds for enterprises which implement devices or processes securing a reduction in emissions of harmful substances;
- higher depreciation rates for industrial fixed assets devoted to environmental protection;
- special taxation of environmentally harmful technologies and activities; and
- credit concessions for enterprises irrespective of their form of ownership (*i.e.* including those with foreign investment) which carry out effective protection of the environment.

Chapter 14
Environmental Regulation in Spain

Xavier Junquera and Eusebio Pujol*
Baker & McKenzie, Barcelona

Sources of Environmental Regulation

Constitutional Provisions

The Spanish Constitution of 1978 expressly recognises its citizens' right to enjoy an adequate environment, a right which is balanced with the duty to preserve it. The Constitution gives the authorities the mandate to use natural resources reasonably and to protect and improve the environment (Article 45).

International treaties and conventions are expressly regarded as part of the Spanish legal system once their final text is officially published in Spain (Article 96 of the Constitution). Therefore, Articles 130R, 130S and 130T of the Treaty of Rome (as amended by the Single European Act and the Treaty of Maastricht), are also applicable in Spain.

Legislation

Environmental legislation is by means of general laws enacted by Parliament and royal decrees issued by the government. Legislation is increasing rapidly because of the need to adapt Spanish environmental law to European Community (EC) standards. Apart from specific environmental legislation, general statutes, *e.g.*

---

*The authors gratefully acknowledge the contribution of Xavier Ruiz (Baker & McKenzie, Barcelona) to this chapter.

the Criminal and Civil Codes, include provisions on liability for actions harmful to the environment.

Regulations

Regulations on specific environmental matters are approved by the competent ministry, which until 11 May 1996 was the Ministry of Public Works, Transportation, Telecommunications and the Environment ("Ministry of Public Works") by the issue of ministerial ordinances, irrespective of the legislative powers of other regional, provincial or local bodies or agencies. After the general elections held in March 1996 the Conservative Government created the Ministry of the Environment as proof of the increasing concern for environmental protection.

Relationship between National, Regional and Local Regulation

Spain is administratively divided into 17 regions, called autonomous communities (*Comunidades Autónomas*). These autonomous communities, in addition to the municipalities, have powers to legislate on environmental matters, which can be more restrictive than national legislation. Broadly speaking, the autonomous communities have exclusive competence over matters such as land use and planning, housing and the protection of wildlife and mountain areas. They are also competent to adopt legislation to protect and regulate the use of the environment but within the framework and under the guidelines established by national legislation. Municipalities are competent, by local ordinances, to regulate certain environmental matters, including water supply and collection, recycling and disposal of waste, sewage networks and treatment of waste water.

The development of environmental legislation differs from one autonomous community to the other. Thus, whereas Catalonia is the most advanced in terms of environmental legislative initiatives and its government is considered to be the strictest in the enforce-

178

ment of environmental law, autonomous communities such as Andalucia, Extremadura or Murcia are still at an early stage.

The existence of these administrative divisions has often resulted in confusion and overlapping of competencies, especially between the state and each autonomous community. The situation has been aggravated by the partial delegation by the autonomous communities and municipalities of their powers to government or private agencies and companies.

This outline covers national legislation only, although references are made for illustrative purposes to legislation by autonomous communities and municipalities.

Entities

The most significant entities with powers to legislate, supervise, control or advise on environmental matters are:

- The Environmental Advisory Board (*Consejo Asesor de Medio Ambiente*), which is attached to the Ministry of Public Works and advises the government on environmental matters. The Environmental Advisory Board has among its officials qualified representatives of non-governmental organisations.
- The recently created Ministry of the Environment (*Ministerio de Medio Ambiente*), which assumes the functions of the former State Secretariat for the Environment, formerly a department of the Ministry of Public Works. The Ministry of the Environment is structured as three bodies: (a) the State Secretariat for Waterways and Coasts; (b) the Secretariat General for the Environment; and (c) the Subsecretariat for the Environment.
- The National Water Council (*Consejo Nacional del Agua*), which is a body created by the Water Act (see below) but has not yet been set up. It has an advisory function, and the Water Act attached it to the Ministry of Public Works.
- The River Basin Agencies (*Organismos de Cuenca*), which are the so-called Hydrographic Confederations (*Confederaciones Hidrográficas*), attached to the Ministry of the Environment. They are in charge, amongst other matters, of the preparation

179

of the hydrologic plan for each main river basin, the granting of authorisations to use the public water domain and the collection of waste discharge fees.

- The autonomous communities, which tend to develop their environmental policies through various government entities and agencies. For instance, in Catalonia, water policy is implemented through a Water Council (*Junta d'Aigiles*) and a Water Sanitation Council (*Junta de Sanejament*). Broadly speaking, the Water Council designs the regional government's policy to organise and exploit water resources, while the Water Sanitation Council is in charge of constructing, promoting and controlling the infrastructure for the discharge and elimination of residual water. Another example is the Waste Council (*Junta de Residus*), whose main function is to promote and control the facilities for the treatment and elimination of solid or liquid waste.
- The municipalities, most of which have delegated their powers to private or government companies.

Specific Legislation and Regulations Applicable to Certain Areas of Environmental Regulation

Urban Planning Overview

Urban planning law is basically composed of (a) the Law on Soil, enacted by Decree 1346/1976 of 9 April 1976; (b) The New Law on Soil and Urban Planning, enacted by Royal Legislative Decree 1/1992 of 26 June 1992; (c) The Administrative Regulation on Management of Zoning Provisions, enacted by Decree 3288/1978 of 25 August 1978; (d) The Urban Planning Regulations, enacted by Decree 2159/1978 of 23 June 1978; and (e) The Urban Disciplinary Regulations, enacted by Decree 2187/1978 of 23 June 1978. The New Law on Soil and Urban Planning of 1992 modifies important aspects of the Law on Soil of 1976. Nevertheless, its application has been refused in some autonomous communities, such as Catalonia, where its own Soil and Urban Planning Regulations apply, and some other autonomous communities have also implemented their own urban planning laws.

The urban planning laws and regulations seek to regulate the processes of real estate development, the exercise of rights arising from real estate property and the protection of the environment and the natural resources through the prevention of urban mismanagement. The law divides the land into categories of urban land, land to be developed and land not allowed for real estate development.

These categories allow different kinds of land use and real estate development:

Urban Land is land on which the infrastructure works are completed and therefore it is considered already developed and ready for construction purposes. The urban planning regulations approved by each municipality ("Zoning Local Ordinances") precisely define the rights of owners of land in this category (*i.e.* they set out in detail the degree and kind of construction allowed on each plot, such as housing or industrial). Since the Zoning Local Ordinances contain such detailed regulations for such land, in general no further planning is necessary. However, further planning may be necessary, by special urban plans, to improve certain aspects of the infrastructure of urban land, such as waste water disposal.

Land to be developed is land which according to the Zoning Local Ordinances is to be converted into urban land. The ordinances divide the area to be converted in different sectors. The real estate development of each sector must be established in detail by an urban plan (the "Partial Plan"). Partial Plans specify the public services and infrastructure which must be established in each sector, such as green zones, hospitals, schools, roads and areas for housing projects. Partial Plans also determine the land use allowed upon each sector as well as the surrender of land required from landowners to provide the municipality with enough space to establish new public services and infrastructure. This surrender of land is considered part of the landowners' contribution in return for the grant of development rights on their land through the approval of urban plans.

Land not allowed for real estate development is the kind of land that the Zoning Local Ordinances of each municipality protect and assign to uses other than for building, such as agriculture, farming, forestry and protected areas; estate development is generally not allowed.

Air Quality

The basic statute on air quality is Law 38/1972 of 22 December ("Air Pollution Act"), which is however, to some extent obsolete. The Air Pollution Act has a two-pronged approach: first, it establishes air quality standards and second, it sets the maximum permissible emission levels of polluting substances. However, under the Air Pollution Act, these standards and levels are not regarded as absolute and must be balanced against the social benefits involved (*e.g.* employment and economic growth). Thus, if the polluting activities meet the requirements of the Air Pollution Act but public health is nevertheless adversely affected to such an extent as to offset such social benefits, the polluting activities may be banned. Similarly, the Air Pollution Act provides that air quality requirements must be balanced against factors such as the economic cost and technical feasibility of compliance, as well as the effects on the economic development of the regions or areas exposed to the polluting activities.

The Air Pollution Act was subsequently implemented by Decree 833/1975 of 6 February 1975 ("Air Pollution Regulations") which also provide the technical rules for measuring emission levels. The methods to be used for the analysis and measurement of pollutants were provided by the Ordinance of 10 August 1976. Following the distinction established by the Air Pollution Act, the Air Pollution Regulations set out the specific air quality standards and maximum emission levels for polluting substances. These parameters may vary depending on the activities involved. Penalties for non-compliance with the statutory quality requirements range from small fines to a temporary close-down of the factory, irrespective of any criminal, tort or other liabilities under the applicable law. To avoid undue hardship for the employees of a factory which has been closed down, the Air Pollution Regulations provide for the application of the labour legislation by means of an "urgency procedure".

Spain

While the Air Pollution Regulations seek to prevent and reduce air pollution in general, regardless of its origin, the Ordinance of 18 October 1976 was designed to prevent and reduce air pollution of industrial origin only. This ordinance deals with air pollution activities from manufacturing processes in general, as well as related or supplementary services, such as waste incinerators and storage areas. However, the ordinance expressly excludes from its scope pollution caused by radioactive substances. This ordinance requires any activities regarded as polluting the air under the Air Pollution Regulations to be authorised by the Ministry of Industry and it regulates the authorisation procedure before that Ministry and the control and follow-up mechanisms available. The General Directorate of Industrial Promotion and Technology, an agency within the Ministry of Industry, is empowered to supervise and verify that the companies authorised to pursue certain air polluting activities, comply at all times with the requirements of the Air Pollution Regulations and the Ordinance. This directorate also has advisory and supervisory functions. Like the Air Pollution Regulations, the ordinance imposes penalties for infringement of its standards and requirements.

Several regulations have been enacted for the purpose of controlling the use of specific polluting substances. For instance, Royal Decree 1613/1985 of 1 August 1985 (as amended by Royal Decree 1321/1992 of 30 October 1992) regulates the maximum permissible level of sulphur dioxide concentration in the air and the procedure to be followed in case of an emergency. Royal Decree 717/1987 of 27 May 1987 establishes the maximum emission levels for nitrogen and lead dioxide, adopting the EC rule and in part modifying the Air Pollution Regulations.

On 14 October 1978 Decree 2512/1978 was issued in order to give companies incentives to adopt anti-polluting measures by subsidies, tax deductions, low interest loans and free amortisation of loans and credits.

To implement EC Directive 88/1609, Royal Decree 646/1991 of 22 April 1991 (as amended by Royal Decree 1800/1995 of 3 November 1995) sets out new provisions on the limitation of the emissions into the air of certain polluting substances from large combustion facilities, which implies a partial amendment of the Air Pollution Regulations. Royal Decree 1088/1992 of 11 September 1992 implements EC Directives 89/369 and 89/429 on emissions into the air of certain polluting substances from urban waste incineration facilities. Royal Decree 1494/1995 of 8 September 1995 implements EC Directive 92/72 by establishing a survey and information exchange system on ozone pollution to be operated by the different government bodies.

Water Quality

Continental Water

The framework legislation on water and waste water is Law 29/1985 of 2 August 1985 ("Water Act"). The Water Act regulates the use of water and establishes the jurisdiction and powers of the various government bodies involved.

To protect public water, the Water Act generally forbids, *inter alia*, direct or indirect discharge and storage of any solid waste or substances that may pollute water and its surrounding environment. Discharges can be made directly or indirectly into water beds, soil, ponds or excavations, whether by means of discharge, injection or storage. Any activity that may cause discharge into public water requires a government authorisation setting out the applicable conditions and limits. The discharge authorisations contain: (a) a reference to the purifying facilities required and the elements of control of their operation; (b) the limits and parameters of the composition of the effluent; and (c) the fees payable for the authorisation. Any establishment or change in or relocation of any facilities or industries that may cause discharge will be authorised by the authorities only if a discharge authorisation is obtained. The government may prohibit in certain areas those activities and industrial processes, the effluents of which despite treatment carry a serious risk of contaminating water, whether under normal or exceptional working conditions.

The River Basin Agencies (*Organismos de Cuenca*), may suspend the authorisation to discharge on a temporary basis or modify its conditions: only the government may suspend the authorisation definitively.

Authorisations to discharge may be revoked if their conditions are not met. In cases of serious pollution of public water the revocation may be accompanied by withdrawal of the concession to use the water, without any right to compensation to the affected party.

The government may also order the suspension of the activities giving rise to unauthorised discharges or take the necessary measures to remedy such discharges, without prejudice to the liabilities which may have arisen from such discharges.

The Water Act allows companies to be formed to carry on the treatment of waste water produced by third parties. Their discharge authorisations must include the following in addition to those required for all discharges: (a) the acceptability of the discharges to be treated by the company; (b) the maximum prices to be set and the method for their updating; (c) the provision of a bond to guarantee the continuance and effectiveness of the treatment.

Re-use of purified waters

The Water Act requires the government to establish the basic conditions for the direct re-use of waters, taking into account the purifying processes, their quality and the uses envisaged.

In case the re-use is to be carried out by a person different from the primary user of the water, the use and the re-use shall be considered independent of each other and shall be subject to different concessions.

Fees payable for the discharge authorisation

Any discharges authorised under the Water Act are subject to payment to the corresponding River Basin Agency of a fee destined for the protection and improvement of the corresponding river basin.

Water quality standards and parameters

The Water Act was implemented on 11 April 1986 by Royal Decree 849/1986 ("Water Regulations"). This legislation is very comprehensive (having 342 articles) and lays down water quality standards and parameters. For this purpose it establishes two lists of contaminating substances, on the basis of their degree of toxicity. List I (known as the "black list") includes all substances considered specially toxic or with long-lasting toxic effects. The conditions for discharge of black list substances or waste water containing these substances are very restrictive. List II (known as the "grey list") includes less toxic substances, and therefore the discharge authorisation depends on the type or characteristics of the receiving water (*e.g.* whether it is a large river or a public water system). Discharges to aquifers and groundwater of black list substances is strictly prohibited, whilst grey list substances may be discharged under certain conditions.

Water quality controls

Apart from the controls imposed by the relevant authorisation, the River Basin Agencies may undertake appropriate controls and inspections to verify the characteristics of the discharge. This may be done by the River Basin Agencies themselves or by private companies specially authorised for such purpose and listed in a special registry.

Violations and sanctions

The Water Regulations include a classification of violations of its provisions and the applicable sanctions. Since the Water Regulations implement the Water Act and develop its provisions in greater detail, a violation of the Water Regulations would encompass a violation of the Water Act. Furthermore, the relevant provisions in the Water Act on violations and sanctions have been transcribed into the Water Regulations. Therefore, the classification of violations and sanctions in the Water Regulations also apply to the Water Act.

The Water Regulations classify violations as minor, less serious, serious and very serious. Sanctions for these violations may entail withdrawal of the authorisation and the temporary suspension of production. Pursuant to Royal Decree 419/1993 of 26 March 1993 which partially modified the sanctions scheme in the Water Regulations, the fines which may be imposed are the following: (a) minor violations: up to 150,000 pesetas; (b) less serious violations: from 150,001 up to 1,500,000 pesetas; (c) serious violations: from 1,500,001 up to 15,000,000 pesetas; and (d) very serious violations: from 15,000,001 up to 75,000,000 pesetas.

These sanctions may apply irrespective of any potential civil or criminal liabilities. The party responsible for damage to the water environment must compensate any aggrieved party and is required to rectify the damage.

Significant rules enacted for waste water include the Ordinances of the Ministry of Public Works of 12 November 1987, 13 March 1989, 28 June 1991 and 25 May 1992. The Ordinance of 12 November 1987 is the most important, establishing the quality standards under discharge authorisation for various substances (such as mercury and cadmium). The other ordinances expand this list of substances, often to implement EC legislation.

Regulations on discharges

Royal Decree 484/1995 of 7 April 1995 establishes new measures to protect water resources against discharges. The decree implements and expands upon the Water Act and the Water Regulations concerning public water and offers the owners of "irregular" outlets a procedure by means of which they can bring such outlets into compliance. The decree also creates "collaborating entities", which are engineering consultant firms vested with administrative powers to grant official approval to projects for the adaptation of the activities of companies and individuals to the new regulations.

Regulations on waste water treatment

Royal Decree 11/1995 of 28 December 1995 sets out new regulations for the treatment of waste water generated in urban areas. The autonomous communities must establish diverse urban areas within their respective territories in which the decree is to be applied. Each of these urban areas must have its own waste water treatment plant, according to the following schedule:

- by 1 January 1999, urban areas with over 10,000 inhabitants which discharge waste water into the so-called "sensitive zones"; sensitive zones are defined in the decree as the water resources areas defined in future regulations, because of their high degree of pollution or outstanding environmental value, as subject to special protection;
- by 1 January 2001, urban areas with over 15,000 inhabitants;
- by 1 January 2006, urban areas with 2,000 to 15,000 inhabitants.

The waste water treatment plants in urban areas must implement their installations and equipment and use biological treatment systems according to the following schedule:

- by 1 January 1999, urban areas with between 2,000 and 10,000 inhabitants and discharging waste water into sensitive zones;
- by 1 January 2001, urban areas with over 15,000 inhabitants;
- by 1 January 2006, urban areas with 10,000 to 15,000 inhabitants.

By 1 January 2006, plants (a) serving urban areas with less than 2,000 inhabitants and discharging waste water into continental water; and (b) serving urban areas with less than 10,000 inhabitants and discharging waste water into the sea, shall have the appropriate treatment system so that the waste water discharges comply with the legal requirements. Moreover, by 1 January 1999, plants serving urban areas with over 10,000 inhabitants and discharging waste water into sensitive zones shall implement their installations so as to use much stricter treatment systems than biological systems.

The government, after the consultations to be held with the autonomous and local governments involved, will establish the sensitive zones in which the decree is to be applied.

Pursuant to the decree as from 30 December 1995 discharges of sludge into continental water are totally forbidden and as from 1 January 1996 dumping sludge into the sea is also prohibited.

Marine Water

Legislation on marine water quality standards and discharge permitting schemes is found in the Coastal Areas Act 1988 and its implementing regulations. Broadly speaking, this act sets out the limitations and requirements for the discharge of residual water or waste water into the sea, whether from land, ships or aircraft. It also regulates activities on coastal areas such as drilling, excavation and activities causing nuisance.

Pursuant to the Coastal Areas Act, the discharge of solid waste and rubbish into the sea and on the shore is strictly prohibited, unless they may be used as re-fills and this is explicitly authorised.

Any discharge into the sea must be authorised by the competent government body, without prejudice to the need to obtain the relevant authorisation to occupy the marine land zone public domain.

In the case of contaminating discharges, the applicant for any authorisation must justify that there are no better alternatives for the elimination of the waste.

The authorisations must include the terms and conditions under which they are granted including: (a) their term, which may not exceed 30 years; (b) the required facilities for treatment, purification and discharge, including their control systems; (c) the authorised annual volume of discharge; (d) the quality limits of the discharge; (e) an evaluation of the effects of the discharge on the marine water and the water quality objectives of the area involved; (f) the discharge fee, which is assessed taking into account the contamination load of the facilities and using parameters which are very similar to those laid down by the Water Act.

The competent agency may modify the terms and conditions of the authorisation to discharge without compensation to the affected party. This may be done where the circumstances under which the authorisation was granted have varied or where other circumstances occur which would have led to refusal of the authorisation or its grant under different terms. The government may suspend the authorisation until the newly set conditions are complied with. If the party concerned does not implement the modifications required within the period set, the government may cancel the authorisation, without prejudice to any sanctions which may apply. The cancellation of the authorisation to discharge implies the cancellation of the authorisation to occupy the marine land zone public domain.

The competent agency may carry out as many inspections and analyses as it deems necessary to verify the characteristics of the discharge and check the compliance of the conditions imposed in each authorisation.

The Coastal Areas Act was extended by Royal Decrees 849/ 1986 of 11 April 1986 and 927/1988 of 29 July 1988 ("Coastal Areas Regulations"). The procedure to authorise discharges into the sea by marine pipelines is regulated by Ordinance of 13 July 1993.

The Coastal Areas Regulations reproduce the same scheme for authorisations to discharge as that of the Coastal Areas Act, although it is more precise in some respects.

The Coastal Areas Regulations provide, whereas the Coastal Areas Act does not, that when the importance or complexity of the treatment plant so requires, the authorisation to discharge may require that the management of the plant be undertaken by a competent technician or that a specialised company cooperating with the government takes part in its maintenance (together with the submission of periodical certificates on its functioning) or that its activities be insured against certain risks.

Violations and sanctions

The Coastal Areas Act classifies the possible violations of its provisions as serious and minor.

The sanction for any violation of the Coastal Areas Act is a fine:

• Serious violations: for unauthorised discharges up to 50,000,000 pesetas.

- Minor violations: for unauthorised discharges half of what would be imposed for the violation had it been classified as serious but not more than 10,000,000 pesetas.

In case of persistent serious violations, the government may also declare the party concerned prohibited from obtaining concessions and authorisations for a period from one to three years.

If the violation constitutes a criminal offence, a criminal sanction may be imposed and no administrative sanction may apply.

Irrespective of whether administrative or criminal liability is imposed, the infringing party must restore the coastal environment damaged and, if this is not possible, must compensate for the damage. If the infringement consists of the failure to comply with the conditions of the relevant authorisation, the authorisation may be cancelled.

The Coastal Areas Regulations essentially reproduce the scheme of sanctions and the classification of the violations set out in the Coastal Areas Act and establish criteria to calculate the fines to be imposed. In the case of unauthorised discharges of waste water, the amount of the fine must be calculated taking into account the cost of the treatment which would have been imposed had the authorisation been granted. The Coastal Areas Regulations also require that the infringing party returns to the government all profits unlawfully obtained.

The Coastal Areas Regulations also establish some criteria to calculate the amount of the compensation to be made for damage caused by the unlawful activity. The criteria are: (a) the theoretical cost of restoration of the damaged environment; (b) the value of the damaged assets; (c) the cost of the project or the activity causing the damage; (d) the profit obtained as a result of the infringing activity.

Regulations on discharge of dangerous substances into the sea

Royal Decree 258/1989 of 10 March 1989, on general regulations on discharge of dangerous substances from land into the sea, implements EC Directives 76/464 and 86/280. This decree:

- establishes the requirements for the discharge of dangerous substances into the sea (Annex II to the decree sets out the substances the discharge of which into the sea must be regulated by it);

- sets out a procedure to check compliance with the discharge regulations;
- regulates the introduction of programmes to avoid or eliminate pollution by the specified dangerous substances.

Any discharge from land into the sea requires prior authorisation, to be granted by the relevant autonomous community. Such authorisation lays down the terms and conditions of its grant and must be reviewed every four years.

Where waste water containing any of the specified dangerous substances is treated in a plant, the maximum permissible polluting limits may be measured at the point where such waste water leaves the treatment plant, provided the autonomous community so authorises.

Waste Generation

The basic statute on waste is Law 42/1975 of 19 November 1975 ("Waste Act") which seeks to regulate the "collection and treatment of solid urban waste", as stated in its title. However, its scope is broader than its title suggests and it covers any waste produced by: (a) domestic uses; (b) commercial or service activities; (c) hospital/health activities; (d) road cleaning and sanitising; (e) disposal of furniture, utensils, vehicles or dead animals; and (f) industrial, agricultural, construction activities or works and waste which must be collected and disposed of by the municipalities pursuant to regulations.

The Waste Act sets out some essential rules for the production, transportation and disposal of waste. It provides for joint liability for the producer of waste with any unauthorised carrier or manager of such waste.

The Waste Act was revised to conform to EC legislation on 13 June 1986 by Royal Decree 1163/1986. This statute fundamentally extends various definitions and reallocates powers among the environmental bodies and agencies. Under the Waste Act the local authorities are responsible for the collection and treatment of waste, but the producer must bear the expenses of the service. The local authorities may grant two permits for the use and operation of waste dumping facilities and for the industrial use and exploitation of waste. The legal owner of the waste (*i.e.* the producer) has the right of first refusal over the use and exploitation of the waste. The government can order the modification of waste treatment facilities or even expropriate them if public interest so demands.

The framework statute on hazardous and toxic waste is Law 20/1986 of 14 May 1986 ("Toxic and Hazardous Waste Act"). "Toxic and hazardous" waste is defined as any solid, semi-solid, or liquid materials, and any gases in containers which: (a) are the result of a production, transformation, use or consumption process; (b) of which the producer has disposed; and (c) contain any substance defined as toxic and hazardous in a list of 29 substances under the act, in amounts or concentrations sufficient to cause a risk of harm to human health, natural resources or the environment. The rules applicable to toxic and hazardous waste extend to containers, but do not apply to radioactive waste, mining waste and discharges into the air.

Any new industries or activities that generate or import toxic or hazardous waste require an authorisation from the competent agency within each autonomous community. The application for this authorisation must be supported by a technical report on the consequences and correcting measures to treat the waste. The competent agencies may also require the producer to obtain appropriate insurance coverage.

Generally speaking, the conditions which must be fulfilled by waste producers are the following:

- Toxic waste must be contained in suitable safety drums to prevent any leakage.
- Drums containing toxic waste must be properly labelled. The size of the labels must be 10 × 10 cm. and must indicate: (a) a code identifying each waste; (b) the name, address and telephone number of the waste producer; (c) the date of putting into the drums; and (d) possible risks arising from each waste.
- Toxic waste cannot be stored for more than six months. Store

premises must be equipped with waterproof flooring and secondary lining to prevent underground leakage.

- Toxic waste production must be registered in an official book provided and sealed by the environmental authorities.
- Toxic waste producers must submit to the environmental authorities a complete waste report every year. Official forms established by the authorities must be used for this report. The report must indicate the amount, type and origin of both the waste that has been collected and the waste that remains stored.
- Toxic waste must be collected and transported to a specific plant to be treated and eliminated by an authorised company. In any waste collection, the authorised company must issue a certificate stating the amount, type, origin and destination of the collected waste. Waste producers must keep these certificates for at least five years.
- Any disappearance, loss or leak of toxic and hazardous waste must be reported to the relevant agency.

The Toxic and Hazardous Waste Act also makes the management of waste (including treatment, storage, recycling and disposal) subject to a specific authorisation and the keeping of a register. Waste management companies must have an adequate safety and emergency plan. The transportation of waste requires a document identifying the waste carried.

Penalties for violation of the Toxic and Hazardous Waste Act include fines up to 100 million pesetas (approximately US$1 million) and the closing down of facilities or the cessation of production in the event of very serious offences. The relevant agencies may also impose "positive" fines of up to one third of the fine imposed. These penalties are in addition to any criminal liability or civil liability to compensate for damage to an aggrieved party or liability to restore damage to the environment.

The Toxic and Hazardous Waste Act was implemented by Royal Decree 833/1988 of 20 July 1988 ("Toxic and Hazardous Waste Regulations"). As in the case of the Waste Regulations, the Toxic and Hazardous Waste Regulations set out the technical parameters applicable to the production (including bottling and labelling), transportation, storage and disposal of toxic and hazardous waste and regulate in more detail the obligations of producers, carriers and managers of waste. The Toxic and Hazardous Waste Regulations contain schedules and charts to be used to identify the type and distribution of waste and production activities, as well as samples of the forms to be used by producers and managers of waste to file the annual report on toxic and hazardous waste and by carriers to allow the relevant agencies to control the waste.

Royal Decree 937/1989 of 21 July 1989 established the rules for companies and individuals to obtain public subsidies to implement facilities at their industrial facilities to minimise the generation of waste. Pursuant to the decree, companies can be granted subsidies up to 15% of the amount they may invest in: (a) waste management technology; (b) implementation of waste recycling systems; and (c) use of "environmentally friendly technologies".

To implement EC law on follow up and control of transfrontier transportation of hazardous waste, the Ministry of Public Works issued the Ordinance of 12 March 1990 whereby EC Directives 78/319, 84/631, 85/469, 86/121, 86/274 and 87/112 were transposed into Spanish law. These directives set out the rules to be followed by hazardous waste transport companies and producers in terms of: (a) notification of the characteristics of the waste cargo to the authorities of the countries through which the cargo is to be transported; (b) documentation to be completed and filed with the authorities; (c) acknowledgement of receipt to be issued by the country's authorities; and (d) follow-up measures to control the cargo during its transportation. In addition, by a Resolution of 28 April 1995 the National Plan for Hazardous Waste was approved by the government. The plan establishes the objectives and measures to achieve compliance by companies and public administrative bodies with EC law in this area.

Products Classified as Dangerous

Commercial dealing in products classified as dangerous must comply with certain requirements set out in Royal Decree 363/1995 of 10 March 1995 enacting the Administrative Regulation on Notice of New Substances and Classification, Placing in Containers and Labelling of Dangerous Products.

The decree requires dangerous products (such as chemical

products) to be analysed in suitable R&D facilities to determine the risks which the products might cause to human beings and to the environment. The data from such analyses must be notified to the Ministry of Health. The notification, which must include specific information required by the decree, is a prerequisite for the product to be legally placed on the market.

Environmental Permitting Schemes

Procedures

For any commercial or industrial activity, an authorisation must generally be obtained from the relevant authorities. This authorisation is known as the opening licence and is regulated under Decree 2414/1961 of 30 November 1961. It is granted by the municipality of the place where the establishment is to be located or the activity undertaken. The activity must be in accordance with the uses allowed by the urban plan governing the land upon which the establishment is to be set up.

To obtain the opening licence, the applicant must submit an application to the mayor, together with a technical proposal (including maps of the plant or premises), a technical report describing the production activities and their possible adverse impact on the environment and the technical measures to minimise or eliminate these negative effects, including safety measures. The opening licence must be submitted along with the works licence for review and authorisation by the town council of the proposed location of the facility.

The application for an opening licence must be dealt with within four months from the date of filing. If no response is received within this time, the applicant may file a formal request for the decision, and if no decision is made, unless otherwise established in specific legislation, the licence is deemed to be granted, provided that the applicant has been previously granted the works licence to build the facilities. Other permits are required for specific matters, such as disposal of waste, discharge of residual water to sewage, drilling and use of sewers. Such specific permits must be applied for to, and granted by, the Environmental Agency with jurisdiction in each field of environmental protection, depending on the administrative organisation of each of the autonomous communities.

Enforcement of Environmental Regulation

National

Enforcement of environmental regulation used to be mainly through public awareness campaigns (especially by certain autonomous communities) and through the imposition of administrative fines and criminal and civil liabilities deriving from the Criminal and the Civil Codes respectively.

Spanish courts have been traditionally reluctant to impose criminal liability on polluters and other infringers of environmental law, but the Supreme Court decision of 30 November 1990 in the Cercs case appears to reverse this trend. Indeed, the Supreme Court imposed criminal liability with a prison sentence on the technical director of a heavily polluting plant in the province of Barcelona. Other decisions of lower courts followed the Cercs decision. However, with the entry into force of the new Criminal Code as from 24 May 1996, some significant new features for environmental protection by criminal sanctions are introduced.

The former Criminal Code was clearly unsuitable for environmental protection and only referred to environmental crimes in two articles. The new Code aims at more stringent environmental protection and defines the different environmental crimes in seven articles, apart from other articles considered to be ancillary or related to them.

The main features of the new Criminal Code are as follows:

- Sanctions become more severe. Imprisonment for environmental crime now ranges from six months (or even two years if public health is seriously affected) to four years.
- The list of activities resulting in environmental crime and the list of the places or objects which may be affected by such activities have been increased.
- Serious infringement of administrative environmental laws or

regulations is a prerequisite for criminal sanctions to be imposed. Therefore, a person acting within the scope of administrative laws or regulations will not incur environmental criminal liability.

- An environmental crime may be committed simply by causing a risk to the environment. This means that actual damage is not a prerequisite to environmental criminal liability.

As for administrative liability, the laws, administrative regulations and ordinances regulating each area of environmental protection (*i.e.* water, air and land) establish the fines that environmental agencies can impose on those who do not comply with the applicable environmental regulations and cause damage to the environment. These fines may amount to double the value of the damage caused, and also give rise to the infringers' obligation to restore the damage. Administrative law sets forth administrative liability for the persons (either corporate or individual) responsible for any damage or violation of laws and regulations.

As for civil liability, the Civil Code contains certain provisions (*e.g.* Articles 1902 and 1908) which may apply to establish strict or tort liability for any damage caused to individuals and property through actions injuring the environment. In these cases of civil claims based upon environmental law violations brought against several responsible persons, all of them will be deemed jointly and severally liable unless the degree of liability corresponding to each one can be undoubtedly demonstrated. Civil liabilities arising from violations to the environment have a one-year statute of limitation.

Autonomous Communities

The degree of enforcement of environmental regulations by autonomous communities varies depending on the policy and resources of each community. Catalonia and Madrid are taking the lead in this regard. For example, the Catalonian Government has set up a special police department (popularly known as the "environmental patrol") for the purpose of preventing environmental criminal offences. In addition, it has begun a far-reaching policy for the elimination of waste by offering incentives to businesses, creating a "waste products trading market" and constructing waste disposal facilities.

Local Authorities

The municipalities are also increasingly more active in the control and punishment of environmental offenders. However, they have limited technical and human resources available to implement their environmental policies effectively.

Recent Developments and Major Current Initiatives

Information on Environmental Matters

Act 38/95, in force since 14 December 1995, regulates the right of access to information on environmental matters, implementing EC Directive 90/313.

According to the directive, member states must do whatever is necessary to ensure that any person or entity has complete and easy access to information on environmental matters and on the policies held by public authorities, without the need to prove any specific interest in the matter.

Act 38/95 acknowledges the right to have access to information on environmental matters, including the status of water, soil, land, animals, plants and natural areas, as well as any programmes or actions affecting the environment or its protection.

The relevant authorities must provide the requested information within two months of the application, although they may refuse to provide certain types of information listed by the act. The information must be furnished according to the instructions of the applicant, provided it has paid the corresponding fees. Furthermore, the authorities will periodically publish general information on environmental matters.

EC Environmental Management and Audit System

Royal Decree 85/1996 on Environmental Management and Audit, in force since 21 February 1996, sets forth the rules for the application of EC Regulation 1836/93, which allows industrial enterprises to adhere voluntarily to an EC environmental management and audit system.

Pursuant to the EC regulation, companies willing to adhere to this system must: (a) apply policies to evaluate and control the impact on the environment of the operations in the workplace; (b) implement an environmental management programme; (c) carry out or order periodical environmental audits; and (d) issue a public environmental statement, to be made by a certified environmental expert, which will allow the facility of the company to be registered with a special official registry.

Each member state must designate its own relevant authorities to validate the environmental statements of the companies prior to registration, as well as the system to accredit certified environmental auditors. The Spanish government has appointed the ENAC (National Accreditation Office) as the validating and accrediting office. Once an auditor has been validated and accredited, he may act anywhere within the EC, provided that he is supervised by the accreditation entity of each member state. If accredited auditors or agencies fail to comply with the conditions which determined their appointment, such appointment may be revoked.

Contaminated Land Standards

Spanish legislation does not contain clear standards on what must be considered to be contaminated land. However, the Autonomous Community of Catalonia is believed to be developing criteria for classifying contaminated land. It seems that such criteria will take into account the legislation of several EC countries as well as the USA. It is possible that the criteria adopted by this autonomous community will be taken into account for the preparation of similar legislation at a national level.

Chapter 15
Environmental Regulation in Sweden

Bengt Bergendal and Johan Norman
Baker & McKenzie, Stockholm

Sources of Environmental Regulation

Constitutional Provisions

Swedish law, like other Scandinavian legal systems, is essentially a statute law system. The parliament (*Riksdag*) enacts legislation but can delegate to the government the task of making more detailed prescriptions in ordinances.

Since 1 January 1995 Sweden is a member of the European Union. Membership has to a large extent changed the conditions for Swedish environmental legislation. All EC regulations are directly valid and binding to the same extent as national law. Directives on the environment are being gradually implemented. The environmental standards in EC rules are to a large extent present in current Swedish environmental policies. Only those provisions in EC rules which have no parallel in Swedish legislation and require direct legislation or presuppose legislation have been considered as necessary to be transposed to the Swedish legal system. The government or the authority nominated by it may issue directives for environmentally hazardous activities for precautionary measures, which may not be disregarded on the basis of Swedish membership of the European Union.

Statutory texts are usually quoted by year and number in the official series of the Swedish Code of Statutes (*Svensk författningssamling* (SFS)).

Statutes

Regulations aimed at protecting the physical environment can be found in about 200 acts and ordinances.

The central and basic statute is the Environment Protection Act (SFS 1969:387). This has been amended on several occasions, most recently in 1995. The implementing ordinance is the Environment Protection Ordinance (SFS 1989:364).

The Environment Protection Act is a comprehensive statute covering pollution of land and of water (both surface and underground), air pollution and almost all other environmental nuisances (including aesthetic ones; but not radioactivity). However, the Act applies only to stationary sources of pollution, which means that the disturbance must arise from the use of real estate or – in the words of the Act – "from land, buildings or installations".

Another important statute is the Act on Chemical Products (SFS 1985:426). This Act generally applies to chemical substances and compounds. However, the government is empowered to broaden the scope of the Act to specific categories of objects, provided this broadening is necessary for health or environmental reasons. The important part of the act consists of substantive standards. For example, the Act has introduced the principle that if a specific product could be replaced by another product or another technology, etc., resulting in reduced environmental hazards or impact, the first product must not be used. Special ordinances under the Act lay down rules and standards for, among other things, PCBs and pesticides.

The acts mentioned above are so-called framework laws. They provide the general rules and allow or require the government to issue decrees implementing and making specific provisions under these general rules.

As its name suggests, the Environmental Damage Act (SFS 1986:225) establishes the right of persons to compensation from a polluter who causes them damage. The Act imposes obligations to compensate primarily on the strict liability principle. As to causation, the burden of proof is only to a predominant probability. Liability is imposed on those who carry on activities on real estate. The disturbances covered are the same as under the

Environment Protection Act. The Environmental Damage Act provides that a polluter may be liable to pay compensation even though he obtained all necessary permits and acted fully in accordance with them. However, if the disturbances do not exceed what is general usage and usage of the region, compensation is payable only when the damage is caused wilfully or negligently.

The Environment Protection Act contains special provisions for environmental damage insurance. Indemnity is paid from environmental damage insurance to the claimant for bodily injury or material damage covered by the Environmental Damage Act if the claimant is entitled to indemnity but cannot obtain it or if the right to indemnity is statute-barred. Insurance compensation may also be paid on certain conditions if it is impossible to establish who is responsible for the injury or damage. In a special Ordinance on Environmental Damage Insurance (SFS 1989:365), the government has fixed the annual amount payable by anyone carrying on certain environmentally hazardous activities.

Alongside these acts there are special provisions for environmental protection in other legislation. Such rules are to be found, for example, in the Water Act (SFS 1983:291) and in forestry and agricultural legislation. There is also a separate Nature Conservancy Act (SFS 1964:822), which contains provisions for, among other things, the establishment of national parks and regulations for the protection of plants and wildlife. This Act is aimed at protecting the structure of the countryside and providing the public with opportunities for enjoying nature in the form of open-air life and other recreational activities.

Relationship between National, Provincial and Local Regulation

Public administration is carried out not only by the state but also by the 24 county and the 227 municipal authorities. The county administrations (*länsstyrelser*) and the municipal environmental committees implement the environmental statutes and are responsible for their enforcement. They have in many aspects far-reaching competence, *e.g.* in principle each municipality has a right of veto on the use of herbicides in forestry.

Specific Provisions, Statutes and Regulations Applicable to Certain Areas of Environmental Regulation

Air quality

Legislation on air quality is, in principle, based upon the Environment Protection Act, but there are many special statutes as well. Clean air policy is carried out mainly by means of individual examination of each major pollution source.

Special statutes applying to clean air policy are the Automobile Exhaust Act (SFS 1986:1386) and the relevant Ordinance (SFS 1981:1481) and the Act on Motor Gasoline (SFS 1985:838). Also important is the special legislation laying down limits to the sulphur content of fuel oil (SFS 1976:1054 and 1055, 1990:587 and 1990:709).

With the recognition of car exhausts as a major pollution problem, they are to be more closely regulated. Gasoline quality, expecially with respect to lead, is regulated under the Act on Chemical Products. Standards of performance for cars are set under the traffic legislation, since the Environment Protection Act does not apply directly to mobile sources.

Water Quality

Water conservation is regulated mainly by the Environment Protection Act, which applies to, for example, discharge of waste water affecting activities from stationary sources such as industrial plant, population centres and farms. Indirectly, nearly all environmental statutes are significant in this connection, for example the legislation on chemical products.

Waste Generation

The law on the collection and disposal of waste is relatively well developed. Regulations are based on the Environment Protection

Act complemented by the Waste Collection and Disposal Act (SFS 1979:596) and the Act on Environmentally Hazardous Waste (SFS 1985:841).

For final disposition of environmentally hazardous waste as well as for export of such waste special permission is needed.

It is the municipalities that have the responsibility for planning garbage collection and disposal from private households and for general industrial waste.

As a result of legislation in 1993 (SFS 1993:416), the government, or the national authority appointed by the government for the purpose, is empowered to impose a duty on anyone commercially producing, importing or selling a product or a packaging (a producer) to ensure that the waste resulting from such product is removed, re-used, recovered or disposed of in an environmentally acceptable manner. The same applies to a person who, in the course of his commercial activity, produces waste requiring special measures of sanitation or environmental protection. Up to now producers in three areas (packaging, recycled paper and tyres) are responsible for appropriate final disposal of waste.

Environmental Permitting Schemes

Procedures

Swedish environmental regulation is based on a well-developed permit system. Environmentally hazardous activities are subject to approval before being started or altered. The Environment Protection Ordinance lists three categories of activities. The first category comprises enterprises which are the most polluting or likely to cause a nuisance, and these are subjected to examination of the application prior to receiving a permit. The second category, comprising enterprises less likely to cause a nuisance, is only obliged to give notification and needs no permit. Finally, there is "the free sector of activities", not subject to approval but having to meet substantive standards of general application in the law.

Anyone intending to perform an environmentally hazardous activity for which a permit is required shall, before applying for a permit, consult all relevant central and local authorities. The county administration will indicate which other interested parties must be contacted and in what manner before a permit may be applied for.

The Environment Protection Act contains rules governing the conditions under which activities may be carried on. The rules are couched in fairly general terms and provide no fixed criteria for the balancing of impact against benefit.

The examination of applications is comprehensive and thorough. Permit applications must contain among other things:

- the particulars, drawings and technical description required for an assessment of the nature and extent of the environmentally hazardous activity;
- an environmental impact statement which will permit an overall assessment of the effect of the proposed activity on the environment, on health and on the husbandry of natural resources;
- proposals for the protective action or other precautionary measures required to prevent or remedy detrimental effects of the activity; and
- proposals for how the activity should be inspected.

As a basis for the examination of the individual permit applications, use is sometimes made of guidelines from the National Environment Protection Agency, which is Sweden's central environment control authority. These guidelines are not legally binding on the decision makers.

In the case of most applications the National Environment Protection Agency submits a statement on the case to the permit authority.

Entities

Permits under the Environment Protection Act are issued by the National Licensing Board for Environment Protection in Stockholm or by the county administrations. In the Environment Protection Ordinance there are lists indicating which activities are to be examined by which authority.

On activities for which no permission is required but a notification to the authorities is compulsory, a special report is submitted to the Municipal Environment Committee.

The organisation under the Act on Chemical Products is complicated. There is an inspectorate functioning as a central agency. The National Environment Protection Agency has the primary responsibility as regards the ambient environment, whereas the National Board of Safety and Health takes care of occupational hazards and the like. At regional level the county administrations are supervisory bodies, but they also issue certain licences under the Act on Chemical Products. Locally, the public health authorities are supervisors.

Time Periods

The recipient of a permit for an environmentally hazardous activity is in principle entitled to continue the activity for an unlimited time provided it is not extended or otherwise altered.

A permit holder thus runs no risk that the activity will be prohibited. However, new or stricter conditions for the activity can be prescribed ten years after the permit is granted. Such a review may also be made earlier if there has been some radical change in the circumstances.

Enforcement of Environmental Regulation

Supervising authorities are intended to play an important role in enforcing the standards in the Environment Protection Act. The National Environment Protection Agency is the central supervisory authority. The county administrations and municipal environment committees exercise supervision of the individual environmentally hazardous activities.

All environmentally hazardous activities are under the supervision of a supervisory authority. The supervisory authority has the right of access to a factory or other installation and to carry out the inspection required for the purpose of supervision. Anyone conducting environmentally hazardous operations must submit to the supervisory authority the information required about the installation.

The internal control of enterprises is an essential part of enforcement of the regulations and the permit provisions. Every permit is supplemented with an individual control programme which is exercised by the company with periodical reports to and inspection by the supervisory authority. Anyone performing an activity for which a permit has been granted must submit each year a special environmental report to the supervisory body, describing the actions taken to fulfill the conditions of the permit decision and the results of these actions. All supervision costs are borne by the enterprise.

Anyone infringing the regulations of the Environment Protection Act or directives issued in pursuance of the Act is liable to a fine or a maximum of two years' imprisonment. Any natural or legal person disregarding current regulations may also be liable either to an environmental protection fine, corresponding to any profit deriving from the infringement, or to other fines.

Major Environmental Initiatives

A parliamentary committee has in 1996 presented a very extensive draft for new environmental regulation containing *inter alia* a proposal that all EC rules for air quality, water quality, etc. should be regulated by environmental quality standards. The draft is an effort to gather the central enactments on health protection and environment into an environmental code aiming to develop a society which will guarantee a healthy and good environment.

Chapter 16
Environmental Regulation in Switzerland

Daniel Peregrina
Baker & McKenzie, Geneva

Sources of Environmental Regulation

Constitutional Provisions

Switzerland's environmental law is based on several provisions of the constitution.

Article 22quater deals with regional planning and land use, particularly the protection of areas for cultivation, river banks and national monuments.

Article 24bis deals with the protection of water resources, giving the federal government authority to legislate for the rational use and protection of water resources and for prevention of activity damaging such resources.

Article 24sexies gives the federal government the right to legislate for the protection of flora and fauna; the government must also preserve nature and scenic or historic areas.

The main provision is Article 24septies, giving the federal government power to enact all legislation for the protection of the environment.

Article 24novies authorises the federal government to legislate in the area of biotechnology.

Statutes

The federal law on the protection of the environment (FLPE) of October 1983 and the federal law on water protection of January

1991 are the statutes on environmental protection. The FLPE contains provisions on almost all aspects of the protection of the environment, and on the basis of the FLPE the federal government has enacted many implementing decrees covering specific aspects:

- Air Protection of 16 December 1985 amended in November 1991;
- Environmentally Hazardous Substances of 9 June 1986;
- Soil Pollutants of 9 June 1986;
- Movements of Hazardous Wastes of 12 November 1986;
- Protection against Noise of 15 December 1986;
- Environmental Impact Assessment of 19 October 1988;
- Environmental Protection Organisations Entitled to Appeal of 27 June 1990;
- Bottles and Cans of 22 August 1990;
- Waste Management of 10 December 1990;
- Prevention of Major Disasters of 27 February 1991.

The cantons have also enacted regulations implementing the FLPE and its decrees, but mainly determining the authorities competent to execute the tasks prescribed in the FLPE and its decrees. Therefore, Swiss environmental law can be described as basically federal.

The FLPE's implementation of federal decrees is rather detailed, so there is little room for different interpretations from one canton to another. The weight of regulations is greater than that of administrative interpretations, so that the powers conferred on the cantons are limited.

Specific Provisions, Statutes and Regulations Applicable to Certain Areas of Environmental Regulation

Air Quality

Air pollution control is under the FLPE and is based on strict application of the polluter pays principle (Article 2 FLPE) and requires polluters to undertake clean-up measures.

The standards for ambient air quality (emission standards) are very strict and are defined in the Decree on Air Protection. According to the FLPE, emission standards must be determined to protect human health, fauna and flora, biological communities and habitats.

Based on this principle the Decree on Air Protection provides for the following legal instruments:

- emission standards for eight parameters;
- recommendations on uniform analytical methods for measurement of air pollution and their interpretation;
- numerous emission standards which must be applied preventively, irrespective of emission levels;
- an obligation on operators of installations which do not comply with the provisions of the decree to improve these installations within five years; and
- for highly polluted areas, a duty on cantonal authorities to tighten emission limits further and prepare strategic plans for pollution abatement.

The emission limits must be met by both old and new installations, both inside and outside heavily polluted areas. The cantonal governments must also comply with the federal emission standards whenever they grant permits for the construction of installations located in highly polluted areas.

In 1987 the Decree Relating to the Construction and Equipment of Road Vehicles, based on the Federal Road Traffic Act of 19 December 1958, introduced the requirement of one-way catalytic converters for all new cars.

Water Quality

During the 1970s water pollution control was the first systematic joint effort of federal and cantonal authorities in environmental protection. The Federal Act on the Protection of Water Resources from Pollution of 16 March 1955, amended on 8 October 1971, had a substantial protection objective and contained generous provisions for federal funding.

The Decree on Waste Discharge of 8 December 1975 set emission standards for waste water to ensure quality control. As yet there are no provisions for groundwater quality.

The crucial problems for water resources are controlling water pollution from agriculture, eutrophication of surface waters through increased phosphate concentration, locally critical nitrate concentration in groundwater and drinking water and the devastation of river landscapes because of insufficient water flow downstream from river dams.

Therefore, the 1955/1971 legislation was completely revised in 1991. The main provisions of the new federal law are quantitative water protection (*e.g.* ensuring minimum water flow, especially downstream from hydroelectric power plants), protection of water resources in agriculture and measures to be taken to avoid water pollution by hazardous substances. This act entered into force on 1 November 1992.

Waste

Emission limits for waste incinerators have been adopted in the Decree on Air Pollution; in particular, emission limits for heavy metals are strictly defined.

To avoid the creation of dangerous waste, the Chemicals Decree postulates that substances particularly adverse to the environment should, if possible, not be produced at all. Therefore, the decree prohibits the production, introduction, circulation and application of several chemicals (*e.g.* alkaline monocyclic hydrocarbons, halogenated biphenyls, DDT and their derivatives) and provides that for certain other substances (*e.g.* mercury) a special permit may be necessary. The decree also prescribes restrictions for 13 categories of chemical products including detergents, pesticides, defrosting agents, condensers, anti-corrosive agents and synthetics.

The Decree on the Transport of Hazardous Wastes seeks the complete and uninterrupted control of all national or transboundary dealing with hazardous waste: intermediate storage, treatment and final storage. It imposes obligations on waste producers, transporters and receivers. Compliance with obligations is supervised by cantonal authorities or in a case of import and export by federal authorities.

The Decree on Waste Management seeks to ensure the proper management of waste. The priorities for such management are: waste prevention, salvage of waste material and waste disposal as a last resort. Communities must undertake waste separation (paper, glass, aluminium, and organic waste, etc.) This decree also encourages the recycling of re-usable waste material. For the remaining waste, incineration is preferred to dumping. Waste incineration should enable heat recovery or energy generation to take place. Dumping is allowed for inert materials and for hazardous waste that has been fully stabilised by pre-treatment. The Decree on Bottles and Cans requires the producers and importers of beer and soft drinks to use recyclable bottles or packs. In order to avoid federal directives concerning the recycling of used products similar to the decree on bottles and cans the producers and importers tend to organise themselves on a voluntary basis in order to organise the recycling of products; such private organisation exists in particular for the recycling of computers, printers, copiers and other similar hardware.

Noise

Noise abatement policies are based on five principles:

- for new building areas the federal planning standards for noise reduction must be adhered to;
- construction of new installations must comply with planning principles;
- existing installations must comply with the environmental quality standards for noise through medium-term noise abatement measures;
- additional standards must be met for soundproofing of existing and new buildings; and
- areas with noise levels above the alarm level must be given priority treatment (compulsory improvements).

Maximum permissible noise levels are set according to the time of day (daytime/night-time values) and divided into four categories of degree of sensitivity according to the predominant nature of an area (*e.g.* residential, industrial or mixed activities). It is for the cantons to determine the degree of sensitivity applicable to each property.

Noise abatement measures must be completed within 15 years. Cantons must submit noise abatement programmes periodically to the federal authorities. These programmes must list the individual measures that have been taken on the basis of previously established noise pollution maps.

Noise abatement poses technical problems of implementation in coordination with air pollution control, although coordination is desirable, as both policies seek the restriction of private road traffic and also affect public transport.

Soil Protection

To protect the quantity of the soil and secure more economical use of land, the Regional Planning Act of 1979 created obligatory agricultural zones and protection buffer zones. These areas were intended to deal with problems arising from increasing surface salting and loss of arable land.

To protect the quality of the soil the Decree on Pollutants in Soil of 1986 seeks to safeguard an abundance and productivity of fauna and flora, to achieve an unimpaired decomposability of soils, to ensure free growth of indigenous plants and plant communities without human interference and to guarantee that products are compatible with human and animal health. For these purposes the decree sets limit values for 11 metals and requires cantons to monitor soil conditions continuously. If the limits are exceeded, cantonal authorities are to take appropriate abatement measures in the areas of air pollution, environmental chemicals and waste. This decree is not applicable to contaminated industrial areas and does not set any obligation to clean-up contaminated sites.

Industrial Accidents/Disaster Control

To prevent major disasters, any person operating or intending to operate installations or store substances which could in exceptional circumstances seriously damage persons or the environment must

214

take steps to protect them. In particular, suitable sites must be chosen, prescribed safety distances must be observed, technical safety measures must be taken and supervision of the installation and organisation of warning systems must be ensured.

The Decree on the Prevention of Major Disasters of 24 February 1991 requires enterprises using hazardous substances to notify the responsible authority of the types and amounts of the substances used and the safety measures chosen. It authorises the cantonal authorities to impose additional safety measures if necessary.

Environmental Chemicals

Article 26 of the FLPE prohibits the marketing of substances for applications where, when used correctly, the derivatives or waste can endanger persons or the environment.

The Chemicals Decree implementing this provision is based on the principle of self-supervision: producers of chemical substances must carry out an expert assessment of the environmental compatibility of new and, as far as possible, existing substances. For existing substances, authorities may require additional clarification. The results of this assessment, together with the prescribed safety sheets for chemical substances, must be submitted to the relevant authority in an environmental impact statement. The decree contains a number of legal requirements for the exercise of self-supervision. For example, the reports on environmental impact statements may only be prepared by authorised laboratories with attested "good laboratory practice". Obligatory licences for chemicals are the exception; however, use of certain especially hazardous substances is restricted or prohibited. In addition, the legislation contains requirements for packing, labelling and safe use of chemical products which may endanger the environment.

Environmental Permitting Schemes

There are no independent environmental authorisation procedures. Environmental protection must therefore be considered within

215

existing authorisation procedures (such as for building permits) by the federal, cantonal or local authorities. The specific environmental permission is therefore included in the conditions under which these authorisations are issued.

So that the authorisation may take environmental protection into account, the Decree on Environmental Impact Assessment (EIA) requires an assessment for the construction or modification of facilities that may have significant effects on the environment (*e.g.* multi-storey car parks, various kinds of industrial plant and railroads). The decree lists in an appendix about 70 categories of facilities requiring an EIA.

The EIA includes parameters for air, noise and water pollution where there are relevant environmental quality standards. In the future, however, the EIA may also cover soil pollution, nature and landscape conservation, and may take regulations on land-use planning into account. This implies that, in the long run, federal and cantonal authorities may use the EIA as an enforcement instrument in all environmental legislation.

Enforcement of Environmental Regulation

Enforcement of the federal regulations is the responsibility of the 26 cantons. The practice on enforcement varies in intensity and quality because of differences in priorities (in the allocation of resources and the political importance attributed to environmental protection), as well as the degree of centralisation and strictness of enforcement policies.

In order to minimise as far as possible cantonal variations in enforcement, appeal lies to the federal authorities from the decisions of the cantonal authorities in matters involving federal regulations. Environmental protection organisations also have the right to appeal against decisions concerning the planning, construction or alteration of installations requiring an environmental impact assessment.

Infringement of environmental regulations may result in the liabilities set out below.

Civil Liability

Except for the federal law on water pollution control which prescribes strict liability for water pollution, there is no specific
regulation for civil liability for environmental damage.

Liability therefore arises under the general rule applying to
unlawful damage suffered by any victim. Thus, pursuant to the
general rule in Article 41 of the Code of Obligations, any person
or company can be held liable for environmental damage if the
damage is unlawful and was caused wilfully or negligently.
According to case-law on Article 41, anyone creating a hazardous
situation must take all reasonable precautions to prevent damage
to others. Any owner of real estate is liable if he exceeds his rights
of ownership, *i.e.* emits smoke, soot or noxious fumes or causes
noise prejudicial to his neighbours (Articles 679 and 684 of the
Civil Code).

Administrative Liability

The administrative authorities have power to order or undertake
themselves all appropriate measures to prevent or clean up any
serious pollution of the environment. They can deal with either
the entity causing the disturbance or the person responsible for
the condition causing the disturbance. Thus, the purchaser of
contaminated land may be held liable for all contamination of such
property, even though it was caused by a previous user. Nevertheless, according to case-law, the polluter should be held primarily
responsible.

Criminal Liability

Under the FLPE there is criminal liability for breach of the federal
environmental protection regulations, punishable by imprisonment or fine. Since a company cannot be held criminally liable, it
is primarily the directors and management of the company that
may be prosecuted.

In theory, every infringement of the obligations set out in the

FLPE or the federal decree implementing the federal law may be subject to criminal prosecution. Nevertheless, in practice, criminal proceedings are not used by the authorities as a tool to implement environmental law. The risk of criminal prosecution is therefore usually limited to cases of wilful infringement of important environmental obligations or to major environmental disasters.

Major Environmental Initiatives and Proposals

Since the FLPE was enacted in October 1983, the government has considered it necessary to review this legislation completely in view of new developments in environmental protection as well as the development of environmental regulation in the EC. Therefore, on 21 December 1995 parliament passed important amendments to the FLPE. However, because of the need to implement these amendments by new federal decrees, the amendments will enter into force by stages from 1 July 1997 to 1 July 1999.

The main amendments to the existing legislation can be summarised as follows:

Biotechnology

The use and marketing of genetically modified or pathogenic organisms will require a permit from the federal authorities, as will their release for laboratory purposes. If a genetically modified organism is put on the market, the fact of genetic modification must be disclosed to the customer. The federal government is authorised to issue further regulations on the import, export and transport of organisms, further protective measures, further permit requirements and the prohibition of the use of certain organisms.

Waste Management

The federal government is under a duty to regulate the management of special waste, *i.e.* waste requiring special measures for disposal. Management of special waste also requires a permit issued by the relevant canton. Transport and management of special waste must be notified to the authorities. The cantons must plan and notify the federal government of their needs for waste facilities and their capacity to manage waste, and they must cooperate in the planning of management and disposal of waste.

Waste must be disposed of by the holder. Any waste which cannot be allocated to a holder must be disposed of by the cantons. The holder or a canton may have third parties carry out this task. The holder of waste has to pay for the cost of the disposal. If the holder is unknown or unable to pay, the canton must pay. In order to cover the cost of disposal, the federal government may introduce advance disposal fees and require producers and importers to pay such fees to an organisation which has to use the collected fees to finance the disposal of the particular waste concerned. Operators of waste sites have an obligation to provide security by a reserve fund, insurance, or other means for the cost of safeguarding or cleaning up the site.

Supervision of Waste Sites and Other Contaminated Areas

The cantons are under a duty to ensure the supervision and clean-up of waste sites and contaminated sites where there are damaging or noxious emissions or a risk of future emissions. The federal government may regulate the requirements for control. The cantons must establish a public register of waste sites and contaminated sites.

The costs of any necessary measures are to be borne by the polluter. Where there are several contributors to the pollution, the costs will be divided among them. The owner of a waste site or a contaminated site is also liable. However, he may escape from liability if he can show that despite due diligence he did not know of the contamination and that the contamination did not provide him with any economic benefit.

In order to finance the clean-up of waste sites, operators of waste sites may be asked to pay a fee for the storing of waste.

Green Taxes

The introduction into the market by producers of volatile organic compounds (VOC) and of extra-light heating oil with sulphur content of more than 0.1% will be subject to a tax of Swiss francs 5 per kilogram of VOC and Swiss francs 20 per metric tonne of extra-light heating oil. The tax is regarded as an attempt to reduce VOC emissions by 75,000 metric tonnes a year. The funds collected are to be distributed at the discretion of the federal government.

Strict Liability

The owner of a facility posing a special risk to the environment is strictly liable for damage caused by emissions resulting from the realisation of this risk. However, in order to limit the scope of the liability, "environmental damage" is excluded. "Environmental damage" denotes any damage which cannot be allocated to one clearly identified individual or several of them, but only to the public. The amendment to the legislation describes the term "facility posing a special risk to the environment" and provides that the federal government may require the operator of such a facility to secure his liability by insurance or other means.

Cooperation between Authorities and the Business Community

A new feature in Swiss environmental legislation is a duty placed on the federal and cantonal authorities to cooperate with the business community in the implementation of environmental legislation. Effectively, this means that the authorities should promote private initiatives and measures in the business community before implementing decrees, *e.g.* on restrictions on use, advance disposal fees, eco-audits and eco-labelling.

Index

Abatement notices, emissions, 58
Acid waste, pollution control, 15
A Community Strategy for Waste
   Management, 13
Acquisition audits, 110–111
Administrative law,
  Belgium, 29
  Egypt, 48, 53–54
  England and Wales, 56
  France, 83
  Germany, 102–104
  Italy, 125–126
  Netherlands, 144, 151–152
  Poland, 158, 162–163
  Russia, 168–169
  Spain, 178–179
  see also Environmental authorities
Administrative liability,
  France, 83
  Poland, 163
  Spain, 198
  Switzerland, 217
  see also Liability
Advertisements, permitting schemes,
  65
Agence de l'Environnement et de la
  Maitrise de l'Energie (ADEME),
  France, 77
Agency for Environmental Affairs,
  Egypt, 49, 52–53
Agriculture,
  agrochemicals, 51
  Egypt, 51
  England and Wales, 60
  European Community, 4, 14
  herbicides, 51
  Hungary, 122–123

  pesticides, 4, 14
  Russia, 171
  Switzerland, 212
Aircraft, noise pollution, 19–20, 78–79
Air pollution,
  Belgium, 30
  Classified Installations, 76
  Czech Republic, 39–40
  EC framework directive, 8
  Egypt, 49–50
  emissions *see* Emissions
  England and Wales, 57–58
  European Community, 5–9
  France, 76–77
  Geneva Convention, 6–7, 30
  Germany, 91–93
  greenhouse effect, 5
  Hungary, 118–120
  Italy, 126–127
  Montreal Protocol *see* Montreal
   Protocol
  Netherlands, 146
  ozone *see* Ozone
  Poland, 158–159
  Spain, 182–184
  Sweden, 204
  Switzerland, 210–211
  see also Air quality, Pollution control
Airports, taxation, 78–79
Air quality,
  Belgium, 30
  Czech Republic, 39–40
  EC framework directive, 6
  Egypt, 49–50
  emissions *see* Emissions
  England and Wales, 57–58
  European Community, 6–7

France, 76–77
Germany, 91–93
Hungary, 118–120
Italy, 126–127
local authorities powers and duties,
  58
Netherlands, 146
Poland, 158–159
Spain, 182–184
Sweden, 204
Switzerland, 210–211
Altlasten problem, Germany, 101–104
Applications, permitting schemes,
  65–67, 149–151
Appraisal see Environmental impact
  assessments
Appropriate persons, contaminated
  land, 63–64
Aquatic environment see Water
  quality
Aquifers see Groundwater
Arsenic, pollution control, 14, 100
Asbestos, pollution control, 9, 14, 77,
  106
As low as reasonably achievable
  (ALARA), environmental
  damage, 145–146
Assessments see Environmental
  impact assessments
ASSURPOL, France, 85–86
Audits see Environmental audits
Austria, environmental law, 26
Authorisations,
  Classified Installations, 81–82
  fees, 185
  hazardous waste, 193–194
  marine pollution, 189–190, 192
  waste disposal, 130
  water pollution, 184–185
  see also Licensing, Permitting
  schemes

Baltic Commission, 26
Basle Convention on the Control of
  Transboundary Movements of

Hazardous Wastes and their
  Disposal, 17, 26, 52
Bathing water,
  England and Wales, 60
  European Community, 10–11
BATNEEC see Best available
  techniques not entailing excessive
  cost
Belgium,
  administrative law, 29
  air quality, 30
  constitutional law, 27
  contaminated land, 34
  enforcement, 33–34
  environmental information, 29
  environmental law, 27–35
  environmental management, 35
  groundwater, 30–31
  hazardous waste, 32
  liability, 34
  licensing, 28, 30, 32–33
  OVAM, 31–32
  ozone, 30
  permitting schemes, 32–33
  regional decrees, 28
  standards, 29
  surface waters, 30–31
  VLAREM, 28, 32–33
  waste management, 31–32
  water quality, 30–31
Benelux, 29
Best available techniques not entailing
  excessive cost (BATNEEC),
  England and Wales, 57, 65
Bio-fuels, excise duties, 8
Biotechnology, genetically modified
  organisms, 21, 218
Black list, hazardous substances,
  11–12, 31, 186
Boats see Shipping
British Standards Institution, 71
BS7750, 71

Cadmium, pollution control, 12, 92,
  147, 155, 159, 187
Carbon dioxide, pollution control, 6

Index

Carbon monoxide, pollution control, 7

Carbon taxes *see* Taxation

Carbon tetrachloride, pollution control, 5

Cars *see* Motor vehicles

Catalytic converters,
Germany, 93
Switzerland, 211

CFCs, pollution control, 5

Chemical Releases Inventory, 70

Chemicals *see* Hazardous substances, Pollution control

Chicago Convention, 20

Chromium, pollution control, 12, 155

Civil liability,
Egypt, 47–48
England and Wales, 68–69
European Community, 18–19, 23–24
France, 85–86
Germany, 107–108
Hungary, 114
Italy, 132
Netherlands, 148–149, 152–153
Poland, 163–164
Russia, 175
Spain, 198
Switzerland, 217
see also Liability

Classified Installations,
air pollution, 76
authorisations, 81–82
waste management, 79
water pollution, 78

Clean up *see* Environmental damage

Codes of practice, waste disposal, 61

Commission of the European Communities *see* European Commission

Committee for Public Health and Epidemiological Supervision, Russia, 171

Compensation *see* Civil liability

Compliance *see* Enforcement

Conference on Environment and Development (UNCED), 26

Confidential information, environmental information, 70

Consignment notes, hazardous waste, 62

Consistency, enforcement, 68

Constitutional law,
Belgium, 27
Czech Republic, 38
Egypt, 47
England and Wales, 55
France, 75–87
Germany, 89–90
Hungary, 113–114
Italy, 125
Kazakstan, 135
Netherlands, 143
Poland, 157
Russia, 167
Spain, 177
Sweden, 201
Switzerland, 209

Construction industry,
Czech Republic, 42
Egypt, 52–53

Consumer information,
eco-labelling, 23
environmental information, 73
Green Dot scheme, 98–99

Contaminated land,
appropriate persons, 63–64
Belgium, 34
England and Wales, 63–64
France, 80, 82
Germany, 101–104, 111–112
Hungary, 122–123
identification notices, 63
local authorities powers and duties, 63
Netherlands, 148–149
registers, 64
remediation notices, 63–64
Spain, 200
special sites, 63–64
Switzerland, 214, 219

Contributions, waste disposal, 155–156

Index

Controlled waters, pollution control, 59

Council of Europe, environmental damage, 24, 85

Court of Justice of the European Communities *see* European Court of Justice

Courts, England and Wales, 69

Cradle to grave,
hazardous waste, 100–101
waste management, 61, 97

Criminal liability,
Belgium, 34
Czech Republic, 44–45
England and Wales, 68
France, 83–85
Hungary, 114–115
Netherlands, 152
Poland, 164
Russia, 174–175
Spain, 186–187, 190–191, 194, 197–198
Sweden, 208
Switzerland, 217–218
see also Liability

Cyanide, pollution control, 100

Czech Republic,
air quality, 39–40
constitutional law, 38
construction industry, 42
emissions, 39–40
enforcement, 43–45
environmental audits, 42–43
environmental authorities, 39
environmental damage, 37, 43–45
environmental impact assessments, 42
Environmental Institute, 39
environmental law, 37–46
environmental policy, 38, 45–46
Environment Inspectorate, 39
forestry, 42
hazardous waste, 41–42
Hydrometeorological Institute, 39
liability, 43–45
Ministry of the Environment, 39
privatisation, 42–43
surface waters, 40–41
sustainable development, 38
time limits, 44
waste management, 41–42
water quality, 40–41
Water Research Institute, 39

Dangerous materials *see* Hazardous substances, Hazardous waste

DDT, pollution control, 147, 212

Department of the Environment, England and Wales, 56

Detergents, pollution control, 12, 212

Diesel, fuel quality, 8–9

Direction Regionale de l'Industrie, de la Recherche et de l'Environnement (DRIRE), France, 76–77, 79, 82

Disasters,
Egypt, 53
Italy, 131
Russia, 172
Switzerland, 214–215

Discharge consents, water quality, 59–61

Discharges *see* Water pollution, Pollution control

Drinking water, water quality, 10–11, 30, 59

Duales System Deutschland Gesellschaft fur Abfallvermeidung und Sekundarrohstoffgewinnung mbH (DSD), Germany, 98

Dumping *see* Marine pollution

Duty of care, waste disposal, 61

East Germany,
environmental damage, 101–102
environmental law, 91
see also Germany

Eco-Emballages, France, 80–81

Eco-labelling, 23

Eco-management and audit scheme (EMAS), 22–23, 71, 110, 153, 200
see also Environmental audits

Index

Economic incentives,
England and Wales, 72
Poland, 164
Russia, 176
Spain, 183, 195
Eco-taxes *see* Taxation
Effluents *see* Pollution control, Water
pollution
Egypt,
administrative law, 48, 53–54
Agency for Environmental Affairs,
49, 52–53
agriculture, 51
air quality, 49–50
constitutional law, 47
construction industry, 52–53
disasters, 53
emissions, 49–50
enforcement, 48, 53–54
environmental authorities, 49, 52–53
environmental impact assessments,
51–53
environmental law, 47–54
hazardous waste, 52
liability, 47–48
licensing, 51–52
marine pollution, 50–51
noise pollution, 49
radioactive substances, 50
smoking, 50
surface waters, 51
waste management, 52
water quality, 50–51
EMAS *see* Eco-management and audit
scheme
Emissions,
abatement notices, 58
Czech Republic, 39–40
Egypt, 49–50
France, 76–77
fuel *see* Fuel quality
Germany, 91–93
incineration, 212
industrial plants, 8–9, 92–93
installations, 92–93
Italy, 127

Kazakstan, 136–139
local authorities powers and duties,
58
motor vehicles, 7–8, 92–93, 204, 211
Poland, 158–159
Russia, 172
Spain, 183–184
statutory nuisance, 58
Switzerland, 210–211
taxation, 77, 220
waste incineration, 8
see also Air pollution, Pollution
control
Endangered species, Hungary, 115
Energy taxes, environmental policy,
6, 25
see also Taxation
Enforcement,
Belgium, 33–34
consistency, 68
Czech Republic, 43–45
Egypt, 48, 53–54
England and Wales, 67–70
France, 77–80, 82–86
Germany, 102–104, 107–109
Hungary, 114–115, 119–120
Italy, 128–131
locus standi, 68–69, 153
Netherlands, 151–153
notices, 68
Poland, 163–164
proportionality, 68, 103, 152
Russia, 173–175
Spain, 186–187, 190–191, 194,
197–199
Sweden, 207–208
Switzerland, 216–218
targeting, 68
transparency, 68
see also Environmental authorities
England and Wales,
administrative law, 56
agriculture, 60
air quality, 57–58
bathing water, 60
best available techniques not

entailing excessive cost
(BATNEEC), 57, 65
constitutional law, 55
contaminated land, 63–64
courts, 69
Department of the Environment, 56
economic incentives, 72
enforcement, 67–70
Environment Agency, 57, 59–69
environmental authorities, 56–57,
59–69
environmental impact assessments,
70–71
environmental information, 70–71,
73
environmental law, 55–73
environmental management, 71
hazardous waste, 62
Health and Safety Executive, 66
Integrated Pollution Control (IPC),
57, 59–60, 65–66
liability, 56, 68–69
licensing, 61–62
local authorities *see* Local authorities
powers and duties
permitting schemes, 65–67
planning law, 61–63
standards, 60
time limits, 67
transport policy, 73
trespass, 56
waste management, 61–65
water quality, 59–61
English Channel, marine pollution, 12
Environment Agency, England and
Wales, 57, 59–69
Environmental Advisory Board,
Spain, 179
Environmental audits,
acquisition audits, 110–111
Czech Republic, 42–43
European Community, 22–23
Germany, 109–111
see also Environmental management
Environmental authorities,
Czech Republic, 39

Egypt, 49, 52–53
England and Wales, 56–57, 59–69
European Environment Agency, 21
France, 76–77, 79, 82
Germany, 90–91
Hungary, 116–117, 119, 121–122
Italy, 125–126, 131–133
Kazakstan, 136, 138–141
Poland, 158, 160–163
Russia, 168–169, 173–174
Spain, 179–180, 184–185, 198–199
Sweden, 206–207
see also Administrative law
Environmental care systems *see*
Environmental management
Environmental chemicals *see*
Hazardous substances
Environmental damage,
administrative liability, 83, 163, 198,
217
as low as reasonably achievable
(ALARA), 145–146
civil liability *see* Civil liability
criminal liability *see* Criminal
liability
Czech Republic, 37, 43–45
disasters *see* Disasters
East Germany, 101–102
Germany, 101–102
Green Paper on Remedying
Environmental Damage, 19, 24
insurance, 85–86, 172, 203
joint and several liability, 18–19, 44
Kazakstan, 140–141
liability *see* Liability
Lugano Convention on Liability for
Environmental Damage, 24, 85
negligence, 56, 63, 84, 149
nuisance, 56, 58, 63, 152, 205
personal liability, 84
strict liability *see* Strict liability
toxic torts, 69
Environmental impact assessments,
Czech Republic, 42
Egypt, 51–53
England and Wales, 70–71

European Commission, 22
Italy, 131–132
Poland, 161
Russia, 173
Sweden, 206
Switzerland, 216
Environmental information,
  Belgium, 29
  confidential information, 70
  consumer information, 73
  England and Wales, 70–71, 73
  France, 86
  freedom of information, 22, 70–71,
    86
  Spain, 199
Environmental Institute, Czech
  Republic, 39
Environmental law,
  air pollution see Air pollution
  air quality see Air quality
  Austria, 26
  authorities see Environmental
    authorities
  Belgium, 27–35
  compliance see Compliance
  Czech Republic, 37–46
  East Germany, 91
  Egypt, 47–54
  enforcement see Enforcement
  England and Wales, 55–73
  European Community, 1–26
  European Court of Justice, 2–4
  European Parliament, 4
  Finland, 26
  France, 75–87
  Germany, 89–112
  hazardous substances see Hazardous
    substances
  hazardous waste see Hazardous
    waste
  Hungary, 113–123
  implementation of EC directives, 5,
    75–76
  international see International law
  Italy, 125–133
  Kazakstan, 135–142

Maastricht Treaty, 3
Netherlands, 143–156
noise see Noise pollution
Poland, 157–165
pollution control see Pollution
  control
Russia, 167–176
sea see Marine pollution
Single European Act, 2–3
Spain, 177–200
Sweden, 26, 201–208
Switzerland, 209–220
waste management see Waste
  management
water pollution see Water pollution
water quality see Water quality
Environmental management,
  Belgium, 35
  eco-management and audit scheme
    (EMAS), 22–23, 71, 110, 153, 200
  England and Wales, 71
  Germany, 110
  Netherlands, 153, 156
  Spain, 200
  see also Environmental audits
Environmental payments, Kazakstan,
  136–142
  see also Taxation
Environmental policy,
  air quality see Air quality
  Czech Republic, 38, 45–46
  EC treaty rules, 2–3
  energy taxes, 6, 25
  France, 86–87
  free movement of goods, 3–4, 17
  Germany, 111–112
  hazardous substances, 105–106
  Hungary, 115–118
  impact assessment see
    Environmental impact
    assessments
  incentives see Economic incentives
  internal market, 1–2, 4, 15
  Labour Party, 73
  Netherlands, 153–156
  ozone see Ozone

Poland, 165
Spain, 199–200
sustainable development *see*
  Sustainable development
Sweden, 208
Switzerland, 218–220
waste management *see* Waste
  management
water quality *see* Water quality
Environmental Protection Authority,
  Hungary, 121–122
Environmental Protection
  Inspectorate, Hungary, 117
Environment Inspectorate, Czech
  Republic, 39
European Commission,
  A Community Strategy for Waste
    Management, 13
  energy taxes, 6
  environmental impact assessments,
    22
  European Environmental Forum,
    22
  European Waste Index, 14
  Fifth Action Programme on the
    Environment, 1–2, 5
  First Action Programme on the
    Environment, 1, 25
  Green Paper on Remedying
    Environmental Damage, 19, 24
  implementation of directives, 5,
    75–76
  Index of Hazardous Wastes, 14
  Integrated Pollution Prevention and
    Control (IPPC), 24–25
  pressure groups, 68–69
  recommendations, 5
European Community,
  agriculture, 4, 14
  air quality, 5–9
  Belgium, 27–35
  Commission *see* European
    Commission
  Court of Justice *see* European Court
    of Justice
  England and Wales, 55–73

environmental audits, 22–23
environmental law, 1–26
European Environment Agency, 21
France, 75–87
Germany, 89–112
Green Book on the Urban
  Environment, 127
groundwater, 4, 10–11
hazardous waste, 8, 14–17, 62
Italy, 125–133
liability, 18–19, 23–24
marine pollution, 12–13, 26
Netherlands, 143–156
ozone, 5–6
packaging waste, 15–16, 63
Parliament *see* European Parliament
Spain, 177–200
standards, 9–11
surface waters, 10–11
Sweden, 26, 201–208
waste management, 4, 8–9, 13–19
water quality, 4, 9–13
European Court of Justice,
  environmental law, 2–4
European ecological label, 23
European Environment Agency, 21
European Environmental Forum, 22
European Free Trade Association
  (EFTA), 17
European Inventory of Existing
  Commercial Substances
  (EINECS), 20, 105
European Parliament, environmental
  law, 4
European Union *see* European
  Community
European Waste Index, 14
Excise duties, bio-fuels, 8
Exclusion zones, shipping, 13

Federal Environmental Office,
  Germany, 90
Federal Health Office, Germany, 90
Federal Office for Nature
  Conservation, Germany, 90

Index

Federal Privatisation Agency,
Germany, 102
Fees,
authorisations, 185
permitting schemes, 65
Fifth Action Programme on the
Environment, 1–2, 5
Financial incentives *see* Economic
incentives
Finland, environmental law, 26
First Action Programme on the
Environment, 1, 25
Fisheries, water quality, 10–11, 59
Fluorocarbons, pollution control, 40
Forestry, Czech Republic, 42
Foundation for Packaging and the
Environment, Netherlands,
153–154
Framework directives,
air quality, 6
industrial air pollution, 8
waste, 4, 8–9, 13–14
water resources, 10
France,
administrative law, 83
Agence de l'Environnement et de la
Maitrise de l'Energie (ADEME),
77
air quality, 76–77
ASSURPOL, 85–86
constitutional law, 75–87
contaminated land, 80, 82
Direction Regionale de l'Industrie,
de la Recherche et de
l'Environnement (DRIRE), 76–77,
79, 82
Eco-Emballages, 80–81
emissions, 76–77
enforcement, 77–80, 82–86
environmental authorities, 76–77,
79, 82
environmental information, 86
environmental law, 75–87
environmental policy, 86–87
hazardous waste, 79
insurance, 85–86

Integrated Pollution Prevention and
Control (IPPC), 76
liability, 82–86
Ministry of the Environment, 82
noise pollution, 78–79
Nomenclature des Installations
Classees, 81
packaging waste, 80–81
permitting schemes, 81–82
Schemas d'amenagement et de
gestion des eaux (SAGE), 78
Schemas directeurs d'amenagement
et de gestion des eaux (SDAGE),
78
time limits, 83–85
waste disposal, 79–80
waste management, 79–81
water quality, 77–78
Freedom of information,
environmental information, 22,
70–71, 86
Free movement of goods,
environmental policy, 3–4, 17
Fuel quality,
diesel, 8–9
gas oils, 9
petrol, 8–9, 204

Gas oils, fuel quality, 9
Gasoline *see* Petrol
Genetically modified organisms,
biotechnology, 21, 218
Geneva Agreement on Long-range
Transboundary Air Pollution,
6–7, 30
Germany,
administrative law, 102–104
air quality, 91–93
Altlasten problem, 101–104
catalytic converters, 93
constitutional law, 89–90
contaminated land, 101–104,
111–112
Duales System Deutschland
Gesellschaft fur Abfallvermeidung

und Sekundarrohstoffgewinnung
mbH (DSD), 98
emissions, 91–93
enforcement, 102–104, 107–109
environmental audits, 109–111
environmental authorities, 90–91
environmental damage, 101–102
environmental law, 89–112
environmental management, 110
environmental policy, 111–112
Federal Environmental Office, 90
Federal Health Office, 90
Federal Office for Nature
Conservation, 90
Federal Privatisation Agency, 102
groundwater, 95
hazardous substances, 104–107
hazardous waste, 100–101
liability, 107–109
Ministry of the Environment, 90–91
noise pollution, 101
ozone, 93
packaging waste, 97–99
permitting schemes, 92–93
strict liability, 108–109
surface waters, 94–95
time limits, 104
waste disposal, 99–101
waste management, 96–101
waste water, 96
water quality, 94–96
Green Book on the Urban
Environment, 127
Green Dot scheme, Packaging waste,
98–99
Greenhouse effect, air pollution, 5
Green Paper on Remedying
Environmental Damage, 19, 24
Green taxes see Taxation
Grey list, hazardous substances,
11–12, 31, 186
Groundwater,
Belgium, 30–31
European Community, 4, 10–11
Germany, 95
hazardous substances, 11, 186

recommendations, 10
Spain, 186
Guide levels, water quality, 10

Halogenated biphenyls, pollution
control, 212
Havel, Vaclav, 37
Hazardous substances,
black list, 11–12, 31, 186
environmental policy, 105–106
Germany, 104–107
grey list, 11–12, 31, 186
groundwater, 11, 186
industrial plants, 93
radioactive see Radioactive
substances
red list, 59–60
registers, 105–106
Seveso directive, 20–21
Spain, 195–196
Switzerland, 215
transfrontier shipments, 20
water pollution, 11–13
Hazardous waste,
authorisations, 193–194
Belgium, 32
consignment notes, 62
cradle to grave, 100–101
Czech Republic, 41–42
Egypt, 52
England and Wales, 62
European Community, 8, 14–17, 62
France, 79
Germany, 100–101
Hungary, 121
incineration, 8, 17
Italy, 129–130
marine pollution, 191–192
Netherlands, 147–148
Poland, 160
pollution control, 8–9, 14–15
radioactive see Radioactive
substances
Spain, 193–195
special waste, 62
Sweden, 205

Index

Switzerland, 212
transfrontier shipments, 16–17, 101,
    195, 212
HCFs, pollution control, 5–6
Health and Safety Executive, England
    and Wales, 66
Herbicides, pollution control, 51
Hexachlorocyclohexane, pollution
    control, 12, 147
Hungary,
    agriculture, 122–123
    air quality, 118–120
    civil liability, 114
    constitutional law, 113–114
    contaminated land, 122–123
    endangered species, 115
    enforcement, 114–115, 119–120
    environmental authorities, 116–117,
        119, 121–122
    environmental law, 113–123
    environmental policy, 115–118
    Environmental Protection
        Authority, 121–122
    Environmental Protection
        Inspectorate, 117
    hazardous waste, 121
    liability, 114–115
    National Environment Council,
        116–117
    National Public Health Inspectorate,
        119
    noise pollution, 121–122
    time limits, 123
    waste management, 120–121
    water quality, 120
    wildlife, 115, 123
Hydrocarbons, pollution control, 7–8,
    77, 212
Hydrochloric acid, pollution control,
    77
Hydroelectricity, Switzerland, 212
Hydrometeorological Institute, Czech
    Republic, 39

Identification notices, contaminated
    land, 63

Impact assessment see Environmental
    impact assessments
Incentives see Economic incentives
Incineration,
    emissions, 212
    hazardous waste, 8, 17
    municipal waste, 8, 30, 184
    see also Waste disposal
Index of Hazardous Wastes, 14
Industrial plants,
    emissions, 8–9, 92–93
    hazardous substances, 93
Industrial waste, taxation, 80
Information,
    confidential see Confidential
        information
    consumers see Consumer
        information
    environmental see Environmental
        information
    freedom see Freedom of
        information
    registers see Registers
Installations,
    emissions, 92–93
    water pollution, 96
Insurance,
    environmental damage, 85–86, 172
    France, 85–86
    Russia, 172
    Sweden, 203
Integrated Pollution Control (IPC),
    England and Wales, 57, 59–60,
    65–66
Integrated Pollution Prevention and
    Control (IPPC), 24–25, 76
Interministerial Committee for
    Economic Planning, Italy, 132
Internal market, environmental policy,
    1–2, 4, 15
International Agreement on the
    Prevention of Industrial
    Accidents, 21
International law,
    Basle Convention on the Control of
    Transboundary Movements of

231

Index

Hazardous Wastes and their
 Disposal, 17, 26, 52
Chicago Convention, 20
Geneva Agreement on Long-range
 Transboundary Air Pollution,
 6–7, 30
International Agreement on the
 Prevention of Industrial
 Accidents, 21
Lugano Convention on Liability for
 Environmental Damage, 24, 85
Montreal Protocol, 5–6, 30, 40
United Nations convention on
 climate change, 6
Vienna Convention on the ozone
 layer, 30
International Maritime Organisation,
 13
International Organization for
 Standardization (ISO), 71, 110
In Trust for Tomorrow, 73
IPC *see* Integrated Pollution Control
IPPC *see* Integrated Pollution
 Prevention and Control
ISO 14000 series, 110
ISO 14001, 71
Italy,
 administrative law, 125–126
 air quality, 126–127
 civil liability, 132
 constitutional law, 125
 disasters, 131
 emissions, 127
 enforcement, 128–131
 environmental authorities, 125–126,
 131–133
 environmental impact assessments,
 131–132
 environmental law, 125–133
 hazardous waste, 129–130
 Interministerial Committee for
 Economic Planning, 132
 liability, 132
 Ministry of the Environment,
 125–126, 131–132

National Agency for Environmental
 Protection (ANPA), 133
 noise pollution, 128–129
 oil industry, 130
 ozone, 127
 permitting schemes, 132–133
 waste disposal, 129–130
 water quality, 128

Joint and several liability,
 Czech Republic, 44
 European Community, 18–19
 see also Liability

Kazakhstan,
 constitutional law, 135
 emissions, 136–139
 environmental authorities, 136,
 138–141
 environmental damage, 140–141
 environmental law, 135–142
 environmental payments, 136–142
 Ministry of Ecology, 136, 138–141
 privatisation, 140–141
 Regional Environmental Fund,
 139–140
 Republic Environmental Fund,
 139–140
Klaus, Vaclav, 37

Labour Party, environmental policy,
 73
Lakes *see* Surface waters
Land,
 construction *see* Construction
 industry
 contaminated *see* Contaminated land
Landfill,
 taxation, 61, 72, 79–80
 waste disposal, 17–18, 79–80
Large combustion plans, 9, 183
Lead, pollution control, 8–9, 92, 155,
 159, 183
Liability,
 administrative *see* Administrative
 liability

Index

Belgium, 34
civil *see* Civil liability
criminal *see* Criminal liability
Czech Republic, 43–45
Egypt, 47–48
England and Wales, 56, 68–69
European Community, 18–19, 23–24
France, 82–86
Germany, 107–109
joint *see* Joint and several liability
Kazakstan, 140–141
Netherlands, 148–149, 151–153
no-fault *see* Strict liability
personal *see* Personal liability
Poland, 163–164
Russia, 174–176
Spain, 186–187, 194, 197–198
strict *see* Strict liability
Switzerland, 216–218, 220
Licensing,
Belgium, 28, 30, 32–33
Egypt, 51–52
England and Wales, 61–62
Russia, 169–170
see also Authorisations, Permitting
schemes
Limitations *see* Time limits
Local authorities powers and duties,
air quality, 58
contaminated land, 63
pollution control, 66–67, 118, 131,
199, 203
waste management, 162
Locus standi, enforcement, 68–69, 153
Lugano Convention on Liability for
Environmental Damage, 24, 85

Maastricht Treaty, 3
Management *see* Environmental
management
Marine pollution,
authorisations, 189–190, 192
Baltic Sea, 26
bathing *see* Bathing water
Egypt, 50–51
English Channel, 12

European Community, 12–13, 26
hazardous waste, 191–192
North Sea, 12–13
oil industry, 50–51
shipping, 12–13, 50
Spain, 189–192
waste disposal, 13, 50–51, 189
see also Water pollution
Maximum allowable concentration,
water quality, 10
Mercury, pollution control, 12, 106,
147, 155, 187, 212
Methyl bromide, pollution control, 5
Ministry of Ecology, Kazakstan, 136,
138–141
Ministry of Environmental Control
and Natural Resources Protection,
Russia, 170
Ministry of Industry, Spain, 183
Ministry of the Environment,
Czech Republic, 39
France, 82
Germany, 90
Italy, 125–126, 131–132
Poland, 158, 160–162
Spain, 178–179
Montreal Protocol, 5–6, 30, 40
Moscow Environmental Protection
Agency, Russia, 169
Motor vehicles,
emissions, 7–8, 92–93, 204, 211
noise pollution, 19–20
recycling, 99
Municipal waste, incineration, 8, 30,
184

National Accreditation Office
(ENAC), Spain, 200
National Agency for Environmental
Protection (ANPA), Italy, 133
National Board of Safety and Health,
Sweden, 207
National Environment Council,
Hungary, 116–117
National Environment Protection
Agency, Sweden, 206–207

Index

National Fund for Environmental Protection and Water Management, Poland, 165

National Licensing Board for Environment Protection, Sweden, 206

National Public Health Inspectorate, Hungary, 119

National Water Council, Spain, 179

Negligence, environmental damage, 56, 63, 84, 149

Netherlands,
administrative law, 144, 151–152
air quality, 146
civil liability, 148–149, 152–153
constitutional law, 143
contaminated land, 148–149
enforcement, 151–153
environmental law, 143–156
environmental management, 153, 156
environmental policy, 153–156
Foundation for Packaging and the Environment, 153–154
hazardous waste, 147–148
liability, 152–153
packaging waste, 153–155
permitting schemes, 144–147, 149–151
pressure groups, 153
standards, 149
strict liability, 153
waste management, 147–148
water quality, 147

Nile, pollution control, 49, 51

Nitrates, pollution control, 12

Nitrate sensitive areas, pollution control, 60

Nitrogen oxides, pollution control, 6–9, 77, 146, 159, 183

No-fault liability see Strict liability

Noise pollution,
aircraft, 19–20, 78–79
Egypt, 49
France, 78–79
Germany, 101

Hungary, 121–122
Italy, 128–129
motor vehicles, 19–20
Poland, 160–161
Russia, 170
Switzerland, 213–214

Nomenclature des Installations Classees, France, 81

North Sea, marine pollution, 12–13

Notices,
abatement, 58
enforcement, 68
identification, 63
remediation, 63–64
works, 64–65

Nuclear waste see Radioactive substances

Nuisance, environmental damage, 56, 58, 63, 152, 205

Oil industry,
fuel quality, 8–9
Italy, 130
marine pollution, 50–51

Oil spills, pollution control, 13

OVAM, Belgium, 31–32

Ozone,
Belgium, 30
European Community, 5–6
Germany, 93
Italy, 127
Russia, 170–171
Spain, 184
see also Montreal Convention

Packaging waste,
European Community, 15–16, 63
France, 80–81
Germany, 97–99
Green Dot scheme, 98–99
Netherlands, 153–155
PVC, 154

Part A processes, pollution control, 57

Part B processes, pollution control, 58

PCBs, Pollution control, 15, 106

Pentachlorophenol, pollution control, 147
Permitting schemes,
  advertisements, 65
  applications, 65–67, 149–151
  Belgium, 32–33
  England and Wales, 65–67
  fees, 65
  France, 81–82
  Germany, 92–93
  Italy, 132–133
  Netherlands, 144–147, 149–151
  Poland, 158–162
  registers, 65
  Russia, 172
  Spain, 196–197
  Sweden, 205–207
  Switzerland, 215–216
  see also Authorisations, Licensing
Personal liability, France, 84
  see also Liability
Pesticides, pollution control, 4, 14, 104
Petrol, fuel quality, 8–9, 204
  see also Motor vehicles, Oil industry
Planning law,
  England and Wales, 61–63
  Poland, 161
  Spain, 180–182
  waste disposal, 61–63
Poland,
  administrative law, 158, 162–163
  air quality, 158–159
  constitutional law, 157
  economic incentives, 164
  emissions, 158–159
  enforcement, 163–164
  environmental authorities, 158, 160–163
  environmental impact assessments, 161
  environmental law, 157–165
  environmental policy, 165
  hazardous waste, 160
  liability, 163–164
  Ministry of the Environment, 158, 160–162

National Fund for Environmental Protection and Water Management, 165
  noise pollution, 160–161
  permitting schemes, 158–162
  planning law, 161
  State Atomic Agency, 160
  State Inspectorate for Environmental Protection, 160–163
  time limits, 162
  waste management, 160
  water quality, 159
Polluter pays, pollution control, 14, 25, 45–46, 59, 135–136, 203
Pollution control,
  acid waste, 15
  agricultural fuel oil, 60
  agrochemicals, 51
  air see Air quality
  arsenic, 14, 100
  asbestos, 9, 14, 77, 106
  cadmium, 12, 92, 147, 155, 159, 187
  carbon dioxide, 6
  carbon monoxide, 7
  carbon tetrachloride, 5
  CFCs, 5
  chromium, 12, 155
  controlled waters, 59
  cyanide, 100
  DDT, 147, 212
  detergents, 12, 212
  emissions see Emissions
  fluorocarbons, 40
  fuel quality, 8–9
  halogenated biphenyls, 212
  hazardous waste, 8–9, 14–15
  HCFs, 5–6
  herbicides, 51
  hexachlorocyclohexane, 12, 147
  hydrocarbons, 7–8, 77, 212
  hydrochloric acid, 77
  lead, 8–9, 92, 155, 159, 183
  local authorities powers and duties, 66–67, 118, 131, 199, 203
  mercury, 12, 106, 147, 155, 187, 212
  methyl bromide, 5

Index

Nile, 49, 51
nitrates, 12
nitrate sensitive areas, 60
nitrogen oxides, 6–9, 77, 146, 159,
   183
noise *see* Noise pollution
oil spills, 13
ozone, 6, 93, 127, 184
Part A processes, 57
Part B processes, 58
PCBs, 15, 106
pentachlorophenol, 147
pesticides, 4, 14, 104
polluter pays, 14, 25, 45–46, 59,
   135–136, 203
road traffic, 92–93
silage, 60
slurry, 60
sulphur dioxide, 6–7, 9, 77, 92, 159,
   183
suspended particulates, 6–7
titanium dioxide, 4, 15
updating duty, 146
volatile organic compounds, 220
water *see* Water quality
water protection zones, 60
Pressure groups,
   European Commission, 68–69
   Netherlands, 153
Privatisation,
   Czech Republic, 42–43
   Germany, 102
   Kazakstan, 140–141
Proportionality, enforcement, 68, 103,
   152
PVC, packaging waste, 154

Radioactive substances,
   Egypt, 50
   Russia, 171
   transfrontier shipments, 17
Recommendations,
   European Commission, 5
   groundwater, 10
Recycling,
   motor vehicles, 99

waste management, 15–16, 72, 80–81,
   98–99, 130, 154, 205, 213
Red list, hazardous substances, 59–60
Regional decrees, Belgium, 28
Regional Environmental Fund,
   Kazakstan, 139–140
Registers,
   contaminated land, 64
   freedom of information, 70
   hazardous substances, 105–106
   permitting schemes, 65
Remediation *see* Environmental
   damage
Remediation notices, contaminated
   land, 63–64
Republic Environmental Fund,
   Kazakstan, 139–140
Residues, waste disposal, 97, 100
River Basin Agencies, Spain, 179–180,
   184–186
Rivers *see* Surface waters
Road traffic, pollution control, 92–93
Russia,
   administrative law, 168–169
   agriculture, 171
   Committee for Public Health and
      Epidemiological Supervision, 171
   constitutional law, 167
   disasters, 172
   economic incentives, 176
   emissions, 172
   enforcement, 173–175
   environmental authorities, 168–169,
      173–174
   environmental impact assessments,
      173
   environmental law, 167–176
   insurance, 172
   liability, 174–176
   licensing, 169–170
   Ministry of Environmental Control
      and Natural Resources Protection,
      170
   Moscow Environmental Protection
      Agency, 169
   noise pollution, 170

ozone, 170–171
permitting schemes, 172
radioactive substances, 171
State Environment Monitoring
  Service, 173–174
waste management, 169–170
Rylands v Fletcher rule *see* Strict
  liability

Schemas d'amenagement et de gestion
  des eaux (SAGE), France, 78
Schemas directeurs d'amenagement et
  de gestion des eaux (SDAGE),
  France, 78
Sea *see* Marine pollution
Sensitive zones, water pollution, 188
Seveso directive, hazardous
  substances, 20–21
Shellfish, water quality, 10–11
Shipping,
  exclusion zones, 13
  marine pollution, 12–13, 50
  water pollution, 51
Silage, pollution control, 60
Single European Act, 2–3
Slurry, pollution control, 60
Smoke control areas, local authorities
  powers and duties, 58
Smoking, Egypt, 50
Spain,
  administrative law, 178–179
  air quality, 182–184
  constitutional law, 177
  contaminated land, 200
  economic incentives, 183, 195
  emissions, 183–184
  enforcement, 186–187, 190–191, 194,
    197–199
  Environmental Advisory Board, 179
  environmental authorities, 179–180,
    184–185, 198–199
  environmental information, 199
  environmental law, 177–200
  environmental management, 200
  environmental policy, 199–200
  groundwater, 186

hazardous substances, 195–196
hazardous waste, 193–195
liability, 186–187, 190–191, 194,
  197–198
marine pollution, 189–192
Ministry of Industry, 183
Ministry of the Environment,
  178–179
National Accreditation Office
  (ENAC), 200
National Water Council, 179
ozone, 184
permitting schemes, 196–197
planning law, 180–182
River Basin Agencies, 179–180,
  184–186
standards, 186
surface waters, 184–185
time limits, 198
waste management, 192–195
waste water, 188–189
water quality, 184–192
water re-use, 185
Special sites, contaminated land, 63–64
Special waste, hazardous waste, 62
Standards,
  Belgium, 29
  BS7750, 71
  England and Wales, 60
  European Community, 9–11
  ISO 14000 series, 110
  ISO 14001, 71
  Netherlands, 149
  Spain, 186
  Sweden, 204
State Atomic Agency, Poland, 160
State Environment Monitoring
  Service, Russia, 173–174
State Inspectorate for Environmental
  Protection, Poland, 160–163
Statutory nuisance,
  contaminated land, 63
  emissions, 58
  water pollution, 59
Strict liability,
  Czech Republic, 43

England and Wales, 56, 63
European Community, 18–19
France, 85
Germany, 95–96, 108–109
Netherlands, 153
Poland, 163
Sweden, 202–203
Switzerland, 220
see also Civil liability
Sulphur dioxide, pollution control,
 6–7, 9, 77, 92, 159, 183
Surface waters,
 Belgium, 30–31
 Czech Republic, 40–41
 Egypt, 51
 European Community, 10–11
 Germany, 94–95
 Spain, 184–185
Suspended particulates, pollution
 control, 6–7
Sustainable development,
 Czech Republic, 38
 environmental policy, 2
Sweden,
 air quality, 204
 constitutional law, 201
 enforcement, 207–208
 environmental authorities, 206–207
 environmental impact assessments,
 206
 environmental law, 26, 201–208
 environmental policy, 208
 hazardous waste, 205
 insurance, 203
 liability, 202–203, 208
 National Board of Safety and
 Health, 207
 National Environment Protection
 Agency, 206–207
 National Licensing Board for
 Environment Protection, 206
 permitting schemes, 205–207
 standards, 204
 time limits, 207
 waste management, 204–205
 water quality, 204

 wildlife, 203
Switzerland,
 agriculture, 212
 air quality, 210–211
 catalytic converters, 211
 constitutional law, 209
 contaminated land, 214, 219
 disasters, 214–215
 emissions, 210–211
 enforcement, 216–218
 environmental impact assessments,
 216
 environmental law, 209–220
 environmental policy, 218–220
 hazardous substances, 215
 hazardous waste, 212
 hydroelectricity, 212
 liability, 216–218, 220
 noise pollution, 213–214
 permitting schemes, 215–216
 waste management, 212–213,
 218–219
 water quality, 211–212
 wildlife, 214

Targeting, enforcement, 68
Taxation,
 airports, 78–79
 emissions, 77, 220
 energy, 6, 25
 excise duties, 8
 industrial waste, 80
 landfill, 61, 72, 79–80
 waste water, 96
 water use, 77
 see also Environmental payments
Time limits,
 Czech Republic, 44
 England and Wales, 67
 France, 83–85
 Germany, 104
 Hungary, 123
 Poland, 162
 Spain, 198
 Sweden, 207

Index

Titanium dioxide, pollution control, 4, 15
Torts *see* Environmental damage
Toxic materials *see* Hazardous substances, Hazardous waste
Toxic torts, environmental damage, 69
Transfrontier shipments,
  hazardous substances, 20
  hazardous waste, 16–17, 101, 195, 212
  radioactive waste, 17
Transparency, enforcement, 68
Transport policy, England and Wales, 73
Treaty on European Union, 3
Trespass, England and Wales, 56

United Kingdom *see* England and Wales
United Nations,
  Conference on Environment and Development (UNCED), 26
  convention on climate change, 6
Updating duty, pollution control, 146
Urban waste water, water pollution, 12

Vibration *see* Noise pollution
Vienna Convention on the ozone layer, 30
VLAREM, Belgium, 28, 32–33
Volatile organic compounds, pollution control, 220

Waste disposal,
  authorisations, 130
  codes of practice, 61
  contributions, 155–156
  duty of care, 61
  France, 79–80
  Germany, 99–101
  incineration, 8, 17, 30, 184
  Italy, 129–130
  landfill, 17–18, 79–80
  marine pollution, 13, 50–51, 189
  planning law, 61–63

residues, 97, 100
Russia, 169
Sweden, 204–205
Waste management,
  Belgium, 31–32
  Classified Installations, 79
  cradle to grave, 61, 97
  Czech Republic, 41–42
  disposal *see* Waste disposal
  EC framework directive, 4, 8–9, 13–14
  Egypt, 52
  England and Wales, 61–65
  European Community, 4, 8–9, 13–19
  France, 79–81
  Germany, 96–101
  Hungary, 120–121
  local authorities powers and duties, 162
  Netherlands, 147–148
  packaging waste, 15–16, 63
  Poland, 160
  recycling, 15–16, 72, 80–81, 98–99, 130, 154, 205, 213
  Russia, 169–170
  Spain, 192–195
  Sweden, 204–205
  Switzerland, 212–213, 218–219
Waste water,
  Germany, 96
  Spain, 188–189
  taxation, 96
Water pollution,
  authorisations, 184–185
  Belgium, 30–31
  Classified Installations, 78
  Czech Republic, 40–41
  Egypt, 50–51
  England and Wales, 59–61
  European Community, 9–13
  France, 77–78
  Germany, 94–96
  groundwater *see* Groundwater
  hazardous substances, 11–13
  Hungary, 120
  installations, 96

Index

Italy, 128
Netherlands, 147
Poland, 159
sea *see* Marine pollution
sensitive zones, 188
shipping, 51
Spain, 184–192
statutory nuisance, 59
strict liability, 95–96
Sweden, 204
Switzerland, 211–212
urban waste water, 12
works notices, 64–65
see also Water quality, Pollution
   control
Water protection zones, pollution
   control, 60
Water quality,
   bathing water, 10–11, 60
   Belgium, 30–31
   Czech Republic, 40–41
   discharge consents, 59–61
   drinking water, 10–11, 30, 59
   Egypt, 50–51
   England and Wales, 59–61
   European Community, 4, 9–11
   fisheries, 10–11, 59

France, 77–78
Germany, 94–96
groundwater *see* Groundwater
guide levels, 10
Hungary, 120
Italy, 128
lakes *see* Surface waters
maximum allowable concentration,
   10
Netherlands, 147
Poland, 159
rivers *see* Surface waters
shellfish, 10–11
Spain, 184–192
standards, 9–11, 60, 186
Sweden, 204
Switzerland, 211–212
see also Water pollution
Water Research Institute, Czech
   Republic, 39
Water re-use, Spain, 185
Water use tax, France, 77
see also Taxation
Wildlife,
   Hungary, 115, 123
   Sweden, 203
   Switzerland, 214
Works notices, water pollution, 64–65